June 6, 05

Writing for Love and/or Money

For Janet
From her guest
Live Playwright
with thanks
and every good
wish
Frank Gilroy

Writing for Love and/or Money

Outtakes from a Life on Spec

❖ *The Early Years* ❖

FRANK D. GILROY

Smith and Kraus, Inc.
Hanover, New Hampshire

A Smith and Kraus Book
Published by Smith and Kraus, Inc.
177 Lyme Road, Hanover, NH 03755
www.SmithandKraus.com

© 2007 by Frank D. Gilroy
All rights reserved.

CAUTION: The material in this book is fully protected under the copyright laws of the United States of America, and of all countries covered by the International Copyright Union (including the Dominion of Canada and the rest of the British Commonwealth), and of all countries covered by the Pan-American Copyright Convention and the Universal Copyright Convention, and of all countries with which the United States has reciprocal copyright relations.

All rights, including professional, amateur, motion picture, recitation, lecturing, public reading, radio broadcasting, television, video or sound taping, all other forms of mechanical or electronic reproductions such as CD-ROM and CD-I, information storage and retrieval systems and photocopying, and the rights of translation into foreign languages, are strictly reserved. Please contact Smith and Kraus at (603) 643-6431 for any inquiries concerning rights.

Manufactured in the United States of America
Cover and book design by Julia Gignoux
Freedom Hill Design, Cavendish, Vermont
Cover photo of author provided by the author.

The cover photo shows the author poolside, Vegas, 1960

First Edition: September 2007
10 9 8 7 6 5 4 3 2 1

ISBN 978-1-57525-571-2
Library of Congress Control Number: 2007934511

For my sons (Tony, Dan, John) and Ruth who collaborated in their production and almost every other good thing that's happened to me.

We lose — because we win —
Gamblers — recollecting which
  Toss their dice again!

EMILY DICKINSON

When forced to shovel manure,
  do it the best you can
but never call it ice cream.

FRANK D. GILROY

◆ INTRODUCTION ◆

As the man introducing me at the local community college goes on about my loftier achievements and awards, the audience (kids from families straining so they can get a higher education) openly yawns.

Scrapping prepared remarks, I tell them 90 percent of my career has been failure.

"I've been dead broke six times and if I don't sell something soon it'll be seven."

I have their attention.

"In short, I'm a working writer with a family to support who, to make a buck, has written for such TV series as *The Rifleman, Have Gun Will Travel, Wanted Dead or Alive.*"

Having seen these shows via reruns, they react.

Tearing up my speech (to applause) I invite them to ask questions about any aspect of my life that interests them.

Silence.

Then a tentative hand:

"What would you have become if you weren't a writer?"

"A professional gambler."

That surprises and opens the flood gates.

For two hours I'm barraged with nuts-and-bolts

questions about writing: Do I write in longhand? How many hours a day? What's the first thing I ever sold and for how much? How did my parents feel about my trying to be a writer?

These kids aren't interested in what my life is like since I attained a measure of success. What they want to know is how I got there, which might shed light on what they'll have to go through in whatever field they choose.

What follows are some of the things I shared with them and many more, which there weren't time for.

1939

I'm fourteen.

My mother subscribes to *The Saturday Evening Post, Colliers,* and other magazines that print short stories.

I think I can do that.

I write a one-page tale.

Our closest link to literature is my aunt who works in the photo morgue of *The World Telegram.*

She shows my story to a feature writer who reads it and scribbles in the margin: "The boy has narrative ability. Tell him to stay away from journalism."

1940

The ticket seller asks why I'm not in school.

"Poison ivy," I say, displaying my left arm sheathed in one of my mother's long white gloves.

I lose myself in the movie: *City for Conquest* starring Jimmy Cagney and Ann Sheridan.

The music swelling as the lovers (he a blind boxer — she a failed dancer) struggle against overwhelming odds, I experience an electric sense of higher destiny.

The movie over, I remove the glove and exit into the accusing light of another wasted day.

◆ ◆

A man wearing a tuxedo at any time in the Bronx draws attention. That it's mid-afternoon, a weekday, heightens the sense of occasion.

He's Andrew Ponzi, 1940 World Champion pocket billiard player, come to play an exhibition match at the Mount Eden Poolroom.

Admission is one dollar to see Ponzi take on the best local player, in a 125-ball contest. Ponzi's manager — suit and tie — takes Ponzi's cue from its case, screws it together, hands it to the maestro.

The local hero jumps off to a lead.

The lead increases. Are we about to witness a miraculous upset?

Ponzi steps to the table and runs over a hundred balls to win.

Every shot he makes is so short — so simple that I begin to lose respect until I realize making it look easy is what it's all about.

Sensing I've learned something beyond pool, I file it away.

Billy Dietsch, impishly handsome, funny, charismatic, bends the gang (the Panther's AC) to his will without trying.

Learning he can make seventeen dollars and fifty cents a week pressing pants, he quits school. Three guys follow his lead. It would be four if my mother didn't put her foot down.

"You're going to finish high school!" she declares. *"I don't care how but you're going to graduate!"*

Tears streaming, the first demand she's ever made, how can I refuse?

1941

A classmate at DeWitt Clinton High School (ten thousand guys on two shifts) slips me a spicy book — erotic sections marked.

Skipping from one torrid passage to another I become interested in the story and end up reading the whole thing.

Except for *Treasure Island* and *Robinson Crusoe*, *Appointment in Samara* by John O'Hara is the first book I've ever read that isn't a school requirement.

❖ ❖

The wall behind the counter at Lou and Macy Kay's poolroom is increasingly filled with photos of "Our Boys in Service."

There aren't enough guys left for a stickball game.

Billy Dietsch, whose parents signed papers so he could join the navy at sixteen, returns from boot camp. Envious of his uniform and the way everyone regards him, I ask him what it's like.

"Anybody but you, I tell them it's great," he confides. "Just between us, stay out as long as you can."

1942

Wearing one of my father's fedoras and sporting a moustache (courtesy of mother's eyebrow pencil) to look older, I check myself in a mirror before departing for the racetrack.

"You're a bum," my reflection accuses.

"This is the last time," I promise, "Tomorrow I'll turn over a new leaf."

"Do it now."

"Now?"

"Or never!"

Removing the fedora and erasing the moustache, I will myself to the piano where I practice ten minutes of scales, ten minutes of exercises, and ten minutes of a piece — each interval measured by a clock and meticulously recorded in a notebook.

The first one to mark the change is Etta Colin, a faculty member at the Juilliard, who has suffered me as a piano student because she's an old friend of the family.

That I am practicing two hours a day (no more lessons that reduce Etta to tears) astonishes her.

She invites me to play (a first) at her annual recital.

On the home front my mother hasn't had to write a note excusing school absence in several months.

Besides piano and school, I'm trying to become a popular songwriter.

With lead sheets for two of my compositions ("When You Gonna Ring Mr. Mailman?" and "Old-Time Eyes on Broadway"), I inveigle local bandleaders, organists at roller rinks, and whomever I can, to play the songs while my buddy, Lennie McBride, an Irish tenor, sings.

I'm also going to Drake's Business School to learn shorthand and typing.

The first indication that I may be overdoing things suggested when, attending an Eddie Condon jazz concert at Town Hall, I fall in love with Billy Butterfield's solo on "Can't We Be Friends?" and begin trumpet lessons.

❖ ❖

That I'm now practicing the piano four hours a day makes everyone uneasy — especially the Friedmans in the apartment below us.

When I declare my intention of becoming a concert pianist, Etta, feeling she's created a monster, does all she can to dissuade me.

Her efforts in vain, I enroll as a special student (no entrance exam required) at the Juilliard.

I fail music dictation and sight singing — the latter after a re-exam.

My consolation is that Cozy Cole, the great jazz drummer, flunks both outright.

❖ ❖

My father, always secretive about his finances, stuns me: "How would you like to go to Yale?"

Not knowing anyone who's been to college, we assume they take everybody who can ante.

I'm in New Haven to consult the Dean of Admissions about courses. Before I can state the purpose of my visit, he informs I've been turned down.

Pulling into Grand Central, I remember Harry James (whose trumpet sound I seek to emulate) and his band are at the Paramount Theatre.

Am I here to postpone breaking the news to my parents or to savor a temporary defeat that will make ultimate victory that much sweeter?

1943

Stung by Yale's rejection, I work even harder.

Instead of going away with my parents to our summer cottage at Lake Erskine,* I enroll in a Juilliard program in which six-month's work is compressed into six weeks.

For three weeks I put in eighteen- and twenty-hour days trying to keep my head above water.

My mother returns to see how I'm doing. One look and it's off to Doctor Goldberg, who has presided over my sickly body since infancy.

I hear the word *breakdown* as they huddle.

Doctor Goldberg orders immediate rest and gives me a B-12 shot. As I bend forward, fighting nausea, my mother informs him I'll be eighteen in two months and eligible for the draft.

"*Him* in the army?" he guffaws. "Not a chance."

I keep my head down, both insulted and relieved.

Breakdown behind me, two months until my induction physical, I'm working as a messenger for a freight forwarder in lower Manhattan: twenty-five dollars a week, less war-bond deduction, five and a half days a week

I enjoy scampering through the financial district and the piers. What I don't like is the jam-packed subway ride to and fro from work.

This morning, arms pinned to my sides as usual, a

---

* A rustic oasis in New Jersey so different from the Bronx it engenders a split (urban-rural) that never heals.

woman, our noses almost touching, sneezes in my face.

I vow someday to be rich enough to avoid all forms of public transportation.

❖ ❖

Doctor Goldberg's certainty I'll be 4-F making it a mere formality, I report to Grand Central Palace for my physical.

I'm halfway through the assembly line passing from one physician to another.

"What's this about your back?" a doctor asks eyeing the form I filled out.

"I have a sacroiliac condition."

"Touch the floor without bending your knees."

I bend over as far as I can, which leaves a sizeable gap between fingertips and feet.

The doctor places one hand on my neck, the other on my back and pushes. The interval remains. The line of guys behind me clogging, the doctor waves me on.

Another hour of quizzing, prodding, and probing brings me to a room where an officer stamps your paper: "ARMY," "NAVY," or "4-F."

I note a marine sergeant making his way up the line. Reaching me, he stops, takes my papers, quizzes me as he examines them:

"Ever been in jail?"

"No."

"Ever use drugs?"

"No."

"Ever had a venereal disease?"

"No."

Clapping me on the shoulder he says, "Well, Frank, how does it feel to be a marine?"

"I don't want to be a marine."

"Well I'm going to help you," he says escorting me to the head of the line where he plunks my papers on the desk and says, "Here's one."

The officer reaches for a stamp that says "MARINE" as he thumbs my papers. About to stamp them, he hesitates.

"The doctor didn't sign off about your back trouble," he says. "Go and get his signature." As I about-face, the marine sergeant says, "I'll be here all day and there's no other way out of the building."

I recognize the doctor but he doesn't remember me.

"Sacroiliac," I remind.

Uncertain why he didn't sign, he scribbles a note on a pad that authorizes an X-ray.

En route to the X-ray department, I pass the area where they stamp your papers. The marine sergeant is still there.

The X-ray technician takes several shots of my back; he tells me to go to the mess hall and come back after lunch for the results.

I have my first meal on a metal tray, then back to X-ray where the technician hands me an envelope to take to the doctor.

The envelope unsealed, I take a peek:

"Sacroiliac condition within normal limits," written in pencil.

Between the words *condition* and *within* there is sufficient space to insert *not*. It's tempting but fear of the consequences if caught stops me.

Back to the doctor who glances at the report and initials my papers.

A surreptitious look finds the marine sergeant still

there. I return to the mess hall and have a second meal.

I look again.

He's gone!

Rushing to the head of the line, I thrust my papers at the officer with the stamps.

"Army or navy?"

"*Army,*" I assert.

Feeling a hand on my shoulder, I turn in dread.

It's a naval officer wondering why I didn't choose *his* branch.

The memory of being seasick on a fishing boat inspires me.

"My father and grandfather were army men," I lie. "It's a tradition I'd hate to break."

The man at the desk stamps "ARMY" and directs me to a room where I'm sworn in and ordered to report for active duty in three weeks.

❖ ❖

My mother grieves but keeps it to herself.

My father, whose biggest regret is missing out on World War I because he was the sole support of five sisters, his mother, and his crippled father, regards me with surprise, envy, and unprecedented respect.

Doctor Goldberg predicts I won't last a month.

❖ ❖

Lenny McBride intuits the last night before I enter the army will be tough for me and my parents.

Journeying from Brooklyn, unannounced, he appears at our door, sleeps over — a kindness I'll never forget.

1944

Camp Upton.
With 200 other recruits, I'm summoned to an auditorium where a colonel says, "Congratulations men. You've been chosen for air corps training."
Cheers sweep the room.
"Anyone who doesn't wish to avail themselves of this opportunity is free to leave," the colonel appends evoking derisive howls because everyone knows the alternative is the infantry.
As the colonel goes on about becoming pilots, navigators, bombardiers, it hits me with certainty I belong on the ground.
Incredulous looks accompany my exit.

◆ ◆

I abandon the diary I've been keeping because there's too much to record — not just the training but movies and dances, weekend passes; crap games and card games readily available.
Best of all, I'm too far away to referee my parents' endless disputes.
Doctor Goldberg, who said putting me in the infantry was "inhuman" pronounces my adjustment "a miracle."

◆ ◆

I'm in the mechanized Cavalry Reconnaissance Troop of the 89th Infantry Division.
I like the idea of riding instead of walking but the purpose of reconnaissance ("maintaining contact with the enemy") gives pause.

1945

After eleven storm-tossed days aboard the SS *Marine Wolf* we dock in Le Havre. Waiting to disembark, a crap game starts. I break the game — which makes me uneasy because I heard winning big before entering combat is a sign you're doomed.

◆ ◆

Approaching the Moselle River we come upon a dead German soldier, the first we've seen, which indicates the front is near.
There's a steady parade to view him. Some guys go back for second and third looks. Some, like me, don't go at all.
I memorize it for future telling *(The Viewing)*.

◆ ◆

Was there ever a brighter moon — a shallower doorway?
At this moment, standing guard at a farmhouse miles beyond our lines, I may be the most forward element of Patton's Third Army.
Are you listening Doctor Goldberg?

◆ ◆

The road ahead curves gently through a field, enters a forest, disappears.
The lieutenant halts the column, lowers his glasses, signals again.

We proceed more slowly.
Armored car . . . jeep . . . jeep . . . armored car . . . jeep . . . jeep . . . jeep . . . jeep . . . armored car.
The next-to-last jeep is me.
The lieutenant's car enters the woods.
The first jeep follows suit.
My stomach tightens familiarly.
An orange ball appears above the second jeep.
EXPLODES!
Donohue, head thrown back, hands still clutching the steering wheel, looks skeptical — as though he can't believe he's dead.
Saylor expresses concern for his nearly severed leg. His voice tranquil as if he isn't really concerned — just asking to be polite.
A blond, strapping, German youth rises from one of the foxholes that line the road. Hands up, smiling dreadfully, he approaches.
Someone says he's the one who fired the Panzerfaust rocket, killing Donohue and mortally wounding Saylor. Someone guns him down.
Righteous slaughter follows.
If I ever write about it honestly, I'll have to implicate myself.

Words come unbidden.
I send it to the division paper.
My first publication, it begins:

On guard at night in a German town
'Neath the full moon's glow
You begin to feel your watch has stopped.
Christ but the time goes slow.

⬥ ⬥

    The first indication is Sergeant Brody's inability to sleep because he doesn't trust anyone to guard him.
    The second is his shooting at prisoners' feet mindless of ricochets.
    The third is his killing the dog that couldn't be coaxed from a German soldier's lifeless body.
    His sleeve conspicuous where his stripes used to be, he boards the jeep that will take him to headquarters.
    It's the second crack-up in a week.
    My nerves must be better than I thought.

⬥ ⬥

    Mortar shells bracket us.
    Contact with the enemy established we begin the sweet race home.
    Arrive in time to see Dick Powell, the crooner, in a private eye movie. He's surprisingly good. So is Mike Mazurski, who plays a simpleminded brute looking for a girl he loves named Velma.

⬥ ⬥

    "Where we going?"
    "To see a concentration camp."
    "What's that?"
    "I don't know but Eisenhower wants everyone to see it."

⬥ ⬥

Traveling away from the front, there's a sense of holiday till we enter Ohrdruf-Nord, the first concentration camp U.S. troops have encountered.

Naked matchstick bodies piled like cordwood, five and six bodies high.

Lime pits with hands and feet protruding.

Torture racks.

Three men in prison garb, more lifeless than those they survived.

Focusing on one of the bodies (mouth agape as in the middle of a scream), I vow to bear witness.

❖ ❖

The war in its final days. The division is ordered to advance no further.

It's the best of times for everyone except reconnaissance, charged with maintaining contact with the enemy.

Once a day we start down the highway and keep going till we draw fire.

Sometimes five miles. Sometimes fifteen or twenty.

Usual fears compounded by dread of being the last man killed.

❖ ❖

A week after VE Day, a letter from my father informs that Billy Dietsch died of malaria months earlier in a navy hospital.

"I didn't want to tell you until the war in Europe was over."

My sorrow is laced with inevitability: Billy squandered himself as if he knew there'd be no second act.

❖ ❖

Myth has it that when God saw Gmunden, Austria, he so envied its beauty he populated it with terrible people to compensate.

On our way to a New Year's Eve dance, I urge Charlie to memorize the moment as we near the lakeside pavilion from which music and laughter beckon: "We survived the war. We're young. We're healthy. We'll never be so free again."

1946

I meet a sergeant, a college graduate, who edits the division newspaper.

I give him a story I've written.

Over a drink on the day of publication (April 13 — my lucky number) the sergeant/editor, with rueful certainty, says, "You'll be a writer," implying I'll achieve a goal he deeply aspires to but will never achieve.

❖ ❖

Fueled by the GI Bill and a new estimate of myself, I'm determined to go to college.

Two Dartmouth graduates speak of it so rhapsodically, I decide it's where I want to be:

"Dear Dean of Admissions, Dartmouth College,
    I am writing you from Austria where I am on occupation duty after serving in General Patton's

Third Army. I expect to be discharged next spring and would like to apply for admission to Dartmouth in the fall of 1946. Could you please advise me how to proceed?

       Sincerely,
       PFC Frank Gilroy"

"Dear Private Gilroy,
 Enclosed is an application for admission. I am pleased by your interest in Dartmouth but feel it only fair to inform you that we expect no less than five thousand applications for some six hundred places.

       Best wishes,
       Dean Robert Strong"

"Dear Dean Strong,
 My application is enclosed. As you can see my high school grades leave much to be desired. The idea of college never seriously crossed my mind in high school. In the years since, I've undergone a complete turnaround."

"Dear Frank Gilroy,
 I sense your about-face is genuine and applaud you for it. But I would be derelict if I didn't emphasize that your chances of gaining admission are minimal. I strongly urge you not to focus all your hopes on Dartmouth and enclose a catalog of accredited colleges and universities you should consider."

"Dear Dean Strong,
 I appreciate your warning about the slimness of my chances and will apply to other places. But Dartmouth will always be my first choice."

*"Dear Frank,
     I'm touched by your determination and sorry I can't offer you more hope."*

*"Dear Dean Strong,
     In a few days I'll be homeward bound. Would it be possible to visit Dartmouth? I'd like to see it and thank you for your considerate attention."*

*"Dear Frank,
     Interviews can be helpful but high school records carry the most weight. I put this bluntly so you don't contemplate the trip with false hopes or expectations."*

◆ ◆

The SS *Rushville Victory,* 10,000 homeward-bound troops aboard, docks in Staten Island.
    The merchant crew debarks as we look on. The last man down the gangplank is Al who, masquerading as a seaman, paid someone else to do his chores while he ran a nonstop crap game.
    Sailor garb replaced by blue pinstripe suit and tie, it takes a moment to recognize him. When we do, there's a chorused shout of "AL-AL-AL!"
    Al turns and with a sweeping wave, says *"GOOD LUCK BOYS."*
    What an ending if I ever find a story to go with it.

◆ ◆

Having won two grand in an all–Easter Sunday crap game en route home, the black market price for a typewriter is no obstacle.

Someone steers me to the Royal Typewriter office. I ask for Mr. So-and-So.

A small, pale, eye-glassed man greets me furtively — tells me to wait in the corridor.

Several minutes later, he appears with a new Royal portable that he hands me in exchange for a hundred and fifty dollars.

"I'm going to be a writer," I announce grandly.

With a look of supreme disinterest, he vanishes.

❖   ❖

New suit, new shoes, new shirt, new everything, I arrive at Dartmouth.

I didn't tell Dean Strong I was coming because I was afraid he'd discourage me.

Directed to the Admissions Building, I find the door bearing his name. The secretary to whom I state my business blanches:

"Dean Strong died last week," she informs.

❖   ❖

The acting Dean of Admissions examines my records, paints an even darker picture than Dean Strong, offers one ray of light: "Dartmouth doesn't think it's fair to gauge veterans on the basis of college boards."

He gives me the address of the Veterans' Administration in New York where I can take a general intelligence exam.

"But I wouldn't get my hopes up," he cautions.

Figuring I have nothing to lose, I make an impassioned plea:

"I'm a different guy than my school records

suggest . . . I need a break — someone to gamble on me . . . If you let me in and I don't measure up I'll leave voluntarily."

I depart Hanover feeling I'll never see this idyllic place again.

On the train, an attractive WAC (Women's Army Corps) takes the seat beside me in the club car.

"I've always wanted to buy a drink for a serviceman," I say by way of introduction.

But that's another story.

◈ ◈

It's day two of the VA exam.

Yesterday, multiple choice, I feel I did OK but not good enough to compensate for high school grades. Today it's the essay portion that I'm banking on.

I'm the only one taking it.

Well into the second of the two hours allotted, I hear the man overseeing me on the phone with someone named Gladys.

I detect a rendezvous I'm keeping him from — confirmed when he asks me to turn in my paper twenty minutes early.

I refuse.

"Sometimes less is more," he coaxes.

I hold firm.

"I have to go upstairs," he says. "I'll be back by one o'clock. But if by some chance I'm not, put your essay on my table."

◈ ◈

It's five to one and I have a lot more to say.

My gut tells me the supervisor won't return at one or anytime soon.

If I'm right, this could be the break I need. If I'm wrong, so what? Twelve of the colleges I applied to have already rejected me.

I write nonstop for the next hour.

At five to two I put the essay on his desk and exit via the stairs.

At the nearest bar I drink to Gladys.

◆ ◆

August.

I'm getting ready to go to Davis and Elkins in West Virginia, the only college of some twenty applied to that accepted me.

Dartmouth never even bothered to reply.

I arrive home to find my mother in tears; I figure they had another battle.

"You got a letter from Dartmouth," she says. "You've been accepted."

"Where's the letter?"

"Your father has it. He's out taking bows."

1946

"Why are you going to college?" Professor John Finch asks various students the first day of Freshman English.

Some say to get better jobs.

Some say because in their family everyone goes to college.

"To have a happier life," one fellow says.

"That's the answer I've been waiting for," Finch pounces. "You're in the wrong place: The more you learn the more uncertain you'll be about things you've taken for granted."

Slight pause. Then: "The compensation is you'll be unhappier at a higher level of awareness."

❖ ❖

I've passed initial tests in all my courses.
I'm here to stay!
Crossing the deserted campus at three AM after putting *The Dartmouth* ("America's oldest college newspaper") to bed, I emit a shout of exultation.

1947

The movie made from William Saroyan's play, *The Time of Your Life,* starring Jimmy Cagney, prompts me to take a playwriting course.

First assignment: Adapt a short story of your choice into a one-act play.

I select "The Love Nest" by Ring Lardner.

As I type *time, place, at rise,* I have an overpowering sense of déjà vu — know with absolute certainty if there's anything I can do in a superior way, this is it.

1948

Junior year: Managing Editor of *The Dartmouth*; contributor to the literary magazine; occasional guest on the college radio station; several one-act plays produced — a full-length in the offing; trumpet practice and jam sessions.

When I got into Dartmouth, I felt the door to heaven open.

I won't let it close.

❖ ❖

Summer vacation,
A cubbyhole room at the Hotel de Roosevelt in Mexico City.

Music and laughter from the café below entice but I haven't written enough to earn it.

First there is the daily column ("Gilroy Was There") about my experiences in Mexico for the *Concord Monitor* (Concord, New Hampshire). Free of charge because the editor said "Why should I pay you anything when I get Walter Lippman (preeminent syndicated political columnist) for two dollars and fifty cents a week?"

My column completed, I turn to the novella to which I add four pages a day no matter what.

Day's work done, I descend to the café where to the stirring strains of bullfight music by the pianist, I, employing a napkin as muleta and a fork as sword, engage the resident cat in a series of passes producing chorused "OLÉS!"

❖ ❖

Rollicking nights on the town (Alfonse, the café owner, palming me off as a famous American journalist) invariably conclude with the nightcap toast:

"*Una buena aventura sin mala consequencias.*"

"A good adventure without bad consequences."

❖ ❖

An attractive American woman who resides at the hotel (handsome features a little the worse for wear) invites me to have drinks at the bar.
"Do you know who I am?" she challenges after several tequilas.
"No."
Beckoning me close, she confides, "I'm Judy Garland's sister."
Before I can react, Alphonse summons me to a nonexistent phone call.
"*Cuidado hijo,*" he whispers. "She's a Mexican general's mistress."

❖ ❖

I'm taking bullfighting lessons.
When I show promise versus a simulated bull, Alphonse asks them to bring out a small calf for his amigo.
At the risk of invidious comparison to Hemingway, I decline.

1949

I awake in my dormitory bed with my shoes on — recall getting up during the night panicked I was late for the opening tonight of my first full-length play.
When I recount this to Professor Williams, the director, who found my sangfroid during rehearsals unseemly, he's relieved.

One of the minor actors taken ill moments before curtain up, I — the only one who knows the lines — am pressed into service.

Being onstage I experience the full force of a standing ovation — am hooked forever.

❖ ❖

The SS *Tekla*, a Danish freighter on which I'm a passenger, docks in Lisbon.

A telegram awaits informing that I finished ahead of 218 of 221 entrants in a one-act playwriting contest at Valparaiso University in Indiana.

Headier still is the third-place check for thirty-five dollars — my first compensation as a writer.

Drinks on me.

❖ ❖

Budd Schulberg, eminent novelist *(What Makes Sammy Run?)* and screenwriter *(On the Waterfront)* said being editor-in-chief of *The Dartmouth* during his senior year (1936) was the most demanding and responsible job he ever had.

Desperately seeking an editorial subject at two AM (calls from the night editor increasingly frantic), I experience the chilling accuracy of Schulberg's assessment:

Will I be the first editor-in-chief in the history of the nation's oldest college newspaper to come up empty?*

❖ ❖

---

* No.

I'm playing cornet in the Dartmouth Dixieland Band at Zuk's Castle Grill in New Jersey. It's the final night of our post-graduation summer-long engagement during which my dream of becoming a jazzman (and a writer) dies in the face of overwhelming evidence I'm mediocre at best.

Playing beside trombonist Rusty Jackman (Dartmouth '52), whose every solo is a gem he never deigns to repeat, emphasizes my inadequacy.

Knowing it's my last gig, I dig deep — momentarily surpass my limitations.

Bob Pilsbury, ('48) piano player, who's never complimented me, shouts praise.

Before I can thank him he appends: "You sound like Muggsy Spanier."

Spanier, my least favorite trumpet player — it's the coup de grâce.

◆ ◆

Yale Drama School.

I'm here on a twelve-hundred-dollar fellowship from Dartmouth. I reside in a room (seven dollars a week) in Mrs. Freeman's home — bathroom down the hall.

I had six one-act and two full-length plays produced at Dartmouth. I expect to meet classmates with comparable experience — am surprised to learn that the only play most of them have written is the one required for admission.

I'm twenty-six. I have no time to loiter.

I drop all courses except playwriting and focus on the necessity of making a living when the fellowship money runs out.

❖ ❖

Mrs. Freeman appears at my door with a mop.

"Time to get those woolies," she says handing me the day's mail before she begins her weekly cleaning.

The mail includes three more rejection slips for stories sent to various magazines. I add them to a folder: form slips (numerous) separated from the few bearing a comment and/or signature.

Two of today's rejections are form slips. The third appears typed but the signature ("The Editors") on closer inspection is stamped.

I consign it to the form section and reread a couple of the more personal sort for encouragement:

From *Esquire* (10-5-50)

"We found much of interest in 'Re A Comic Principle' but the consensus here seems to be that it is not quite right for our current editorial needs . . . Perhaps you will hit us with something else soon."

From Samuel French (2-2-51):

"We have read and carefully considered A Better Brand of Paint, Then a Month of Rain, *and* What Good's an Icebox Up There, *and are sorry to report we do not feel there would be a sufficient market for these plays . . . However we did enjoy reading them and trust you will let us see your next play when it is ready."*

Both of these, typed and signed, lift my spirits sufficiently to resume work on my first screenplay triggered by word from my father he's made the barroom acquaintance of a man who has a relative in the movie business.

My last day at Yale.
The school year isn't over but the fellowship money's run out; rumor I blew most of it on a horse a gross exaggeration.
I bid farewell to Mrs. Freeman and my friends.
One of whom, from Dartmouth, tells me that in a conversation about who of the aspiring writers at Dartmouth might make it, Professor Finch said, "Gilroy has a shot because his mind's like a manure pile: Always something going on."

1951

Back in the Bronx living with my parents, I write at night and seek employment by day. Rejection slips piling up and nary a nibble of a job.
Lever Brothers turns me down because they feel I'm "too creative."
An agent who expressed interest in my work tells me I'm writing too much — advises me to stop for a while "and let your creative energy reservoir."
A reluctant SOS to the Dartmouth Placement Bureau lands me a job as a messenger at Young & Rubicam Advertising Agency whose president, Sig Larmon, is a Dartmouth alumnus.
The salary is thirty-seven dollars and fifty cents a week.
The first day I'm directed to the firm's library to read the company bible. Halfway through the book it says if your heart really isn't in advertising you'd be well advised to leave immediately.
Necessity demands I resist the urge.

❖ ◆

Friday morning — late summer. A balmy day.

I arrive at Y&R feeling upbeat because I'm meeting friends after work to go off for the weekend. Plus I've composed two sample ads for Y&R clients I can't wait to show to someone in the copy department in my campaign to graduate from the messenger room:

Ad #1: An owl hooting accompanied by voice-over: "White Owl Cigars for the smoker who gives a hoot."

Ad #2: A series of animated stories for Arrow Shirts titled "Shirt Tales."

I appear in the messenger room before anyone but the retired naval chief who runs it.

"Plug in the phone and get the carnation," he directs.

At my blank look, he explains:

"First guy in plugs in the extension phone in the lobby and goes to the florist next door to pick up the carnation that Mr. Larmon always wears and takes it to his secretary."

I proceed to the lobby and plug in the phone.

Then to the florist where I request Mr. Larmon's carnation. As the florist hands it to me, my good feelings surge.

"Give me another one."

"What for?" the florist asks.

"Myself."

I insert the carnation in my lapel and go to Mr. Larmon's office.

His secretary, head bowed, reading, tells me to "Put it there," indicating a counter without looking up. I do so and return to the messenger room where the chief greets me with a look not far from horror:

"Did anyone see you like that?" he demands.

"Like what?"

"Wearing that carnation," the chief says. "Take it off."

I ask why and am told it's an unwritten law at Young & Rubicam that out of deference to Mr. Larmon, no one wears a flower of any sort except him.

"Are you ordering me to get rid of it?" I ask

"No," the chief says. "But if you don't, you're killing your chances."

I tell the chief my Italian grandfather, who came to this country when he was thirteen, often wore carnations. "If I can't wear one, the family hasn't come very far."

The chief, bless his gruff but tender heart, tries to keep me out of harm's way by sending me on one out-of-town trip after another.

As luck would have it, every train's on time and I'm eventually dispatched on errands within the building.

A couple of people wink at me surreptitiously.

One man sidles up and whispers, "Nice going kid."

In the messenger room there's heated debate about whether I'm showing disrespect for a great man.

One messenger, in the minority, says "Because Larmon wears underwear does it mean the rest of us can't?"

As the day progresses, the carnation swells. By late afternoon, to my eye, it's the size of a football.

At last five PM.

I deposit the carnation in the first trash can en route to meeting my friends whom I regale with what happened.

They all praise my stand except one fellow who

says, "It didn't take any courage because you have no intention of staying in advertising."

He's right.

My only regret is not bumping into Mr. Larmon: a carnation-to-carnation encounter that might have provided a fitting denouement.

Advertising behind me (I quit Y&R shortly after the carnation episode), my days are devoted to writing, my nights to grinding out a living as a subsistence gambler at Yonkers Raceway (betting favorites to show in a progressive system that returns forty bucks on a good night).

I keep this hidden from my parents, already concerned about my future.

On his way to work each day my father looks in and says, "Having any luck?"

Days when writing goes well, I shave, shower, and dress neatly to go to the track. Bad days I forgo these things as if to punish myself.

Today's mail brings four rejections. Three of them form. The fourth one, *Esquire,* especially disappointing.

It's attached to a story ("Confessions of Herbert Sokol"), which they'd encouraged me to rework and submit again, it says:

"This still isn't what we want but thanks for the second look."

The new story I'm working on blows up.

Definitely a bad day.

I duck out after supper on some pretext and walk to the Jerome Avenue subway that takes me to the end of the line where a bus, reserved for horseplayers, deposits me at the track.

Between races I spot a face not seen since basic training in 1944.

"*Gottlieb!*" I shout and rush to greet a well-dressed man, ten years my senior, with whom I'd shared the rigors of infantry training and many laughs as we pursued our shared passion for craps and poker.

It takes a long moment for him to recognize me.

"Let's have a drink," I invite.

"I can't," he says. "I'm with friends."

I'm being brushed off, which puzzles until I realize how I must appear to him: unshaven, poorly dressed, race-track setting. The perfect picture of what he thought the crap-shooting kid, known seven years earlier, would become.

As he walks off, I yearn to tell him I've graduated from Dartmouth and attended Yale but refrain.

On the bus from the track to the subway I catch my reflection in the window — realize with a jolt I'm indistinguishable from the motley crew that surrounds me.

I'm back in New Haven because a student director at Yale Drama is doing a one-act play I wrote.

Walking the streets we encounter Drama School students to whom he introduces me as a playwright, which gives a needed lift.

Rehearsals remind me how much I love theater.

On the train back to New York I experience acute melancholy reminiscent of a day I returned to the front after a trip to headquarters where the war seemed light years away.

I locate "Blanche Gaines — Writers' Representative" on the directory.

As the elevator rises I take a swipe at my hair and a deep breath.

Blanche Gaines shares a room with a man selling radio time in Texas, two people selling God knows what, and a lady representing The Italian Renaissance Youth Society.

A pleasant, motherly looking woman, sixtyish, beckons me to a desk occupied by her and a secretary who surrenders her chair.

Mrs. Gaines ("Call me Blanche") is the widow of a radio/television executive whose recent demise compelled her to seek employment after thirty years plus as a housewife.

"I'm only interested in radio and television," she says. "But your stories show a flair for dialogue. Have you ever thought about adapting them into scripts?"

"Tell me which stories you think have the best chance."

She names two. I vow to have the scripts on her desk in a week.

"I take 15 percent until you sell five," she informs. "After that my commission is 10 percent."

Fifteen percent is exorbitant but the matter-of-fact way she says it, as though sales were guaranteed, more than compensates.

About to turn off Greenwich Avenue onto Jane Street, where a blind date awaits, I'm seized by a premonition that stops me in my tracks:

"If I turn this corner my life will be unalterably changed."

I continue to 30 Jane Street where the girl who greets me (Ruth Gaydos) registers as intelligent, witty, and sexy.

So far so good.

We go the Central Plaza where Red Allen, Willie the Lion, J. C. Higgenbotham, Jimmy McPartland et al. reign joyously every Friday and Saturday.

She loves jazz.

Better still.

❖ ❖

Horse handicapping takes time and energy away from writing. This, plus Ruth's curiosity about how I afford cabs and restaurants with no visible means of employment, makes me quit gambling temporarily and launch a fanatic quest to sell something before my money runs out.

❖ ❖

A letter from Blanche informs that one of my scripts found favor at an ad agency where everyone approved purchase until it reached the sponsor.

The story of a father, devoted to mammon, who strenuously objects to his son becoming a violinist, the sponsor vetoes the sale because he has a son who's a violinist, and he, the sponsor, didn't behave that way.

My offer to change the violin to a piccolo falls on deaf ears.

❖ ❖

A cold day — snow forecast.

I accompany Marty Donovan, aspiring songwriter (fellow horseplayer met at Young & Rubicam) as he drops off demo records in the Brill Building.

His rounds completed, we pool our finances: just enough for Romeo's Spaghetti — twenty-five cents for all you can eat — and subway fare to our respective homes in the Bronx and Brooklyn.

We exit Romeo's, surfeit, as snow starts to fall.

Milton Berle emerges from his rehearsal studio next door and is trading quips with adoring fans as he enters the limo that will whisk him to his phenomenally successful TV show.

"I hate him," Marty declares. *"Oh God how I hate him."*

It's not Berle he hates but anyone doing better than us.

About to share my belief that these days of aspiring will be remembered fondly, Marty's curses on discovering a hole in his shoe silence me.

Tap city and no hint of a sale.

My father's "Having any luck?" is tinged with growing doubt.

My upbeat rejoinders sound increasingly hollow.

Blanche hasn't returned recent calls.

My girlfriend's roommate says she's wasting her money paying my way into movies, et cetera.

I seek a job with a friend in the furniture business.

"As soon as you sell a script you'll quit," he says by way of rejection.

That he assumes I'll eventually sell something is more heartening than he knows.

❖ ❖

To speed reaction, I hand deliver a new script to Blanche.
At my urging she reads it on the spot.
"You can do better than this," she says.
In despair I stop at the Grand Central information booth to collect myself, check the clock impatiently to give the impression I'm waiting for someone.
Carols heralding Christmas invite self-pity.
Flash memory of the boys in my platoon who were killed ends it.

❖ ❖

"Have you given any thought to your cabana rental next summer?"
It's my first day at the Atlantic Beach Corporation on Long Island.
I work the phone in an ocean-side shack where four longtime employees of the corporation eye me warily.
If I do well, getting people to renew their leases, I'm promised the assistant manager's job at one of the corporation's three beach clubs this summer. Each club segregated for a different reason: One accepts Jews; one takes Catholics and a few Jews; one is for WASPs only; Blacks verboten at all three. A bitter pill for a guy who as editor-in-chief of the newspaper at Dartmouth struck the first blow against fraternity discrimination via a student referendum.
I call a lady who says she can't renew her cabana rental because she's in the midst of a bitter divorce, which she tells me enough about to make me side with her husband.

I call a man who berates me about a stolen umbrella and seven dollars he mistakenly paid for guest fees yet to be returned.

I call a woman with an asterisk, which I'm later informed means she's persona non grata for hanky-panky with two cabana boys.

At quitting time I retreat to a rented room in Long Beach. A quick bite and then to my typewriter inspired by the glimpse of what my life will be if I fail.

1952

It's been raining for days.

Feet propped on a desk drawer to avoid water rising through the floor, I'm about to make my next cabana call when the phone rings.

"Can you use three hundred and fifty dollars?" a familiar voice asks.

It's Marty Donovan, now employed at NBC, who informs that a ten-minute sketch I wrote has just been purchased for *The Kate Smith Hour*.

❖ ❖

TV listings note that the husband-and-wife team Robert Sterling and Ann Jeffries will appear in "To the Victor" on *The Kate Smith Hour* this afternoon.

I take the day off to see it in person.

Marty and I enter an elevator en route to the studio where *The Kate Smith Hour* takes place. A short, intense man joins us as the doors close.

Marty introduces me to Albert McCleery, producer of the show, noting I'm the writer of today's sketch.

"If I'd read it a second time, I never would have bought it," McCleery snaps.

"Why?" I ask

"No one can say that dialogue."

"I can say it. Want to hear me?"

We ride the rest of the way in silence.

I spot a jazz trombonist (Freddie Ohms) in the studio band, introduce myself saying I'd heard him play at Eddie Condon's.

Sheepish about being found in such a Mickey Mouse setting, he says, "I need to make a living."

I identify myself as the writer of today's sketch adding, "I have to make a living too."

Strains of "When the Moon Comes Over the Mountain," Kate Smith's theme song, opens the show.

Forty-five minutes later and no mention of the sketch, I wonder if my exchange with McCleery made him cancel it.

I think of all the family and friends tuned in.

And then I hear, "'To the Victor' starring Robert Sterling and Ann Jeffries."

Lights up on a sidewalk café. Sterling seated at a table. Nearby a small boy bounces a ball. Sir Elwood appears.

                SIR ELWOOD:
You are David Carter I presume?

                STERLING:
That's right.

                SIR ELWOOD:
I'm Sir Elwood. I want to conclude this unpleasant task as quickly as possible.

Intoxicated by the sound of my words, the ensuing ten minutes are a blur.

I have no idea how it went.

The only thing I'm sure of is that my days as a cabana salesman are over.

❖ ❖

It's three months since I quit the Atlantic Beach Corporation and moved back to my parents' apartment confident I'd soon sell other scripts and get a place of my own.

I count the scripts written and rejected in the interim to assure it isn't lack of effort that's defeating me. That there are thirteen, my lucky number, provides a momentary lift.

❖ ❖

Ruth again paying for restaurants, movies, et cetera.

I open *The New York Times* with extreme reluctance to the "Help Wanted" section.

The phone rings.

"It's a photo between you and a Hollywood writer," Marty informs.

Translation: A sketch submitted to *The Kate Smith Hour* for Arthur Treacher, the quintessential English butler, has made the finals.

"They'll make a decision in an hour." Marty says. "I'll let you know."

Two hours pass. I figure I lost and Marty is loath to tell me.

The phone rings:

"You won by a nose," Marty announces.
I make a ball of the "Help Wanted" section. Aim it at the wastebasket — the championship of the world at stake:
SWISH.

◈ ◈

Despite fear that McCleery wouldn't have bought the sketch if he connected my name to our previous encounter, I attend the broadcast.

Making myself as inconspicuous as possible, I savor audience laughter that owes as much to Treacher's patented delivery as my lines.

I'm about to exit when Marty says Treacher wants to meet me.

It's my first face-to-face with a star of any magnitude.

Treacher says he loved the role (a racetrack tout with a heart of gold), wonders if there isn't more in it to be mined.

Marty and I repair to a luncheonette where we concoct a series in which Treacher plays the role of Harry Crumb.

We get as far as the title ("Harry the Well-Bred Crumb") when we come to our senses.

◈ ◈

At my grandmother's, I happen on a composition book, "Frankie's Stories" penciled on the cover.

I've never seen it before but I know what it is: a record of where my uncle has sent my stories in an effort to market them while I concentrate on TV.

When he volunteered, I said OK as long as he didn't report anything until he sold one or got more than a form rejection.

For eight months he hasn't said a word.

I open the book at random on a page headed "Liquidation," a story that has been turned down by twelve magazines without personal comment. Postage and date sent and returned duly noted.

A hasty scan finds the same dismal report on every page.

I'd tell him to stop but it's one of his few diversions from caring for my crippled cousin, plus his unwavering confidence gives me heart.

❖ ❖

Ruth doesn't mind footing the bill at restaurants and movies. But she's adamant about slipping me cash to maintain the illusion I'm paying.

Tonight's check at Chumley's (five courses for a dollar and a quarter plus wine) totals four bucks.

She proffers a five dollar bill that I decline:

"It's on me," I announce laying a twenty on the table.

"You're gambling again."

"Strike one."

"I give up."

"Remember Everett Sloane who played the editor in *Citizen Kane?*"

"What about him?"

"Three weeks from tonight he and Wendell Corey will co-star in "The Duel" on the *Gulf TV Theatre.*"

Thus do I break the news of my first half-hour sale.

❖ ❖

I arrive in the midst of a run-through: Wendell Corey and Everett Sloane are doing the climactic scene.

Some of the lines are unfamiliar.

I take a script from one of the production aides. The title page says it all:

THE DUEL
by
Frank D. Gilroy and **David Davidson** *(emphasis mine)*

Rushing to Blanche's office, I interrupt a meeting between her and an older writer to vent my rage about the rewrite.

The older writer pulls a pint of whiskey from his raincoat, invites me to take a swig commemorating the loss of my virginity.

❖ ❖

Ruth and I write a children's book called *Little Ego* about a mouse with an identity problem.

My secret fear it might become a huge success, dwarfing anything else I ever write, surges as I read the opening line of the response from Coward McCann:

"This is an extraordinarily good first book."

The rest of the note spelling out why they won't publish it makes me breathe easier while ostensibly sharing my collaborator's disappointment.*

---

* *Little Ego* was published eighteen years later (1970) by Simon & Schuster.

1953

I'm at J. Walter Thompson waiting to see the story editor of *The Lux Video Theatre* about a script of mine they bought. The door to the editor's office opens and a small, distinguished man in a white suit, who registers familiarly, emerges.

As he boards the elevator, it hits me: William Faulkner!

Entering the editor's office I ask what Faulkner was doing here.

"We're doing a story of his on *Lux* the week before yours," he informs.

My meeting, involving minor changes to accommodate the star Josephine Hull, goes smoothly.

As I rise to leave, the editor says, "The week *after* your show we're doing an adaptation of Eugene O'Neill's play, *Isle*.

Faulkner, me, and O'Neill!

So much for those friends who think I'm selling out.

◆ ◆

A call from Blanche in that special voice heralding a sale. Not just a sale but my first hour-length script that will premier a new *Kraft Television Theatre* series.

I take secret delight that the agency that bought *Johnny Came Home* had previously turned it down when it was titled *The Hero*.

Blanche invites me to a cocktail party where I meet other writers who have crossed the line separating those who pay her 15 percent from we hallowed few who now pay 10.

❖ ❖

A three-month drought ends with two scripts bought within forty-eight hours: *One Summer's Rain* to the *Revlon Summer Theatre; A Matter of Opinion* to *Armstrong Circle Theatre.**

I celebrate with an out-of-hock party to which only people I owe money are invited.

A goodly throng overflows Ruth's apartment. The festivities interrupted while I repay each of my creditors with cash.

Marty recites a poem he composed for the occasion that begins:

Success has touched Frank Gilroy
Touched him lightly it is true.
And touched him in a different way
Than he touched me and you.

❖ ❖

My life on hold since my mother was declared terminally ill.

My father goes to work while I tend her.

Doctor Goldberg pays his daily visit to administer a shot.

Mother sleeping, I savor the quiet that will end abruptly when PS 82 lets out.

Something stirs against my will. It's an idea for a western that seems sacrilegious given the situation. The more I resist, the more it blooms. Within minutes I have the entire story including a title: *The Last Notch.*

---

* Both television shows. "Theatre" a misnomer.

⸫

My mother dies as I complete the script — which I accept as her parting gift.

1954

Blanche's voice, announcing the sale of *The Last Notch* to *The U.S. Steel Hour* has a note of added excitement because the show is produced by The Theatre Guild.*

The price (seventeen hundred and fifty dollars less commission) the most I've ever received, Ruth and I decide to marry.

"Don't drive at night," my father says when I break the news and borrow his car for our honeymoon.

It's the fourth piece of advice he's ever given me: "Always wear a rubber," when I entered the army; "You'll never know how much a hundred dollars is worth until you try to borrow it," when I squandered the considerable sum I brought home from Europe; "Never tell a man to shove his business up his ass because it's a hell of a dark place to have to go looking for business."

The latter a dictum he himself never heeded.

⸫

---

* A venerable theater organization trying its hand at TV.

As the clerk at City Hall pronounces us man and wife, he notes the date (February 13) and the time (eleven minutes after eleven).

Could a marriage be launched with fairer augury?

◈   ◈

Lo and behold our honeymoon travels find us in the vicinity of Hialeah.

As we enter the track, I remember Ruth's brother, Joe, handing me two bucks with instructions to play the favorites in the Daily Double should we happen to go to the races.

Joe wins. I kick myself for not playing his hunch, consoled by the paltry payoff: twenty-six dollars.

I fail to cash a ticket all day necessitating an SOS to Blanche to wire two hundred. A slight chill invades our honeymoon chamber: Ruth isn't opposed to gambling — just losing.

She goes to sleep. I reflect on the day:

Suppose instead of favorites, Joe told me to play long shots resulting in a four grand double?

Suppose instead of two dollars, Joe had given me ten to bet resulting in a payoff of twenty thousand bucks?

Suppose Ruth and I were not the honorable duo we are and decided to pocket the money since Joe had no way of knowing when or if we went to the track?

By the time I doze off, I have the nucleus of a script that will more than compensate for the day's losses.

Thus spake Trigorin.

◆ ◆

I'm in a booth with Lawrence Langner, Armina Marshall, Theresa Helburn (the Theatre Guild triumvirate), and representatives of the U.S. Steel Corporation, viewing the dress rehearsal of *The Last Notch,* which will be aired live this evening.

Everything that can possibly go wrong does, climaxed by the hero unable to get his six-shooter out of his holster at the crucial moment.

At the final fade-out, there's a hollow chorus of "Bad dress rehearsal means a great show."

Langner wants me to add a final line he feels will save the day. Rejecting the idea as tactfully as I can, I exit.

In the subway everyone seems to have their newspapers opened so I'm facing large ads proclaiming:

First you saw HIGH NOON
Then came SHANE
Now on TV see THE LAST NOTCH

At breakfast, when I first saw the ad, I was disturbed by the absence of my name. Now I'm enormously grateful.

◆ ◆

Everything that went wrong at the dress rehearsal goes right in the broadcast.

Blanche calls repeatedly:

Columbia Pictures and Warner Brothers want scripts. The Warner's representative noting Mr. Warner had seen it personally, "not the whole show but enough to make him interested."

Houghton Mifflin invites submission of any western novels or stories I have.

William Schuman, composer and president of the Juilliard, wants to turn *Last Notch* into an opera.

The Theatre Guild would like me to turn it into a play.

The hottest writer in Blanche's stable (Rod Serling) phones congratulations from Cincinnati.

Warners calls again — asks how much we want.

Blanche calls the Theatre Guild lawyer for advice. He tells her to ask for "in the neighborhood of forty thousand."

Blanche passes this to the Warner's man who finds it exorbitant. She assures him it's negotiable.

Three more studios ask for a price.

By the third call, Blanche omits "in the neighborhood" pronounces "forty thousand" with confidence. Option offers she dismisses laughingly.

Midnight.

Blanche again.

She feels it's more than she can handle — wants to hire a highly recommended theatrical attorney. If he (Eddie Colton) makes the deal, he gets 3.5 percent. No deal he gets nada.

I approve.

Ten minutes later she calls back. Colton is hired.

First order of business: He tells her to wire everyone to whom she quoted forty grand and cancel it because "We've got a really hot property!"

And so to bed with visions of sugar plums, et cetera.

It's a week since *The Last Notch* aired. No let up in offers fueled by a rave Sunday review in *The New York Times*.

MCA would like to represent me.

Life magazine is interested in doing a spread on me and the show.

Ballantine Books wants to convert it into "a quality western novel."

Famous Artists requests a script for a famous actor they refuse to identify until we say, "No name — no script." It's Kirk Douglas.

H. N. Swanson, a prominent Hollywood agent, is confident he can get me a screenwriting job for one thousand dollars a week. Eddie Colton, given the imminent sale he foresees, derides Swanson's offer.

Mrs. Sam Goldwyn (Frances), who recommended the show to her husband, calls Blanche to arrange a meeting between Mr. Goldwyn and me.

In the midst of these doings, I work on a script for the Kodak Family Adventure series.

Bills must be paid.

◆ ◆

I'm in Sam Goldwyn's waiting room ten minutes early for our appointment.

The receptionist studies a racing form.

At eleven-thirty Mr. Goldwyn enters.

He's distressed he might be late, I assure him I'm early.

Conscious he's the most powerful person I've ever met, I memorize him: square features, well-tanned, erect, alert, energized. Conservatively but elegantly dressed: black homburg, black suit with gray pinstripes.

He talks about a movie he made called *The Westerner* noting it's a "minor classic." He seems interested in a sequel that might involve me. His fractured speech leaves it unclear.

Enter Mrs. Goldwyn who acts as interpreter.

"Frank what Mr. Goldwyn means is . . . " "Sam what the boy is saying is . . ."

Goldwyn states emphatically that he doesn't want to get in a bidding war for *The Last Notch*. Doubtless due to Eddie Colton having sold him *Guys and Dolls* in a blind bidding contest in which (reputedly) the second highest bid was nowhere near Goldwyn's offer.

"Have you made any definite deals?" he asks.

"No."

"How about moral obligations?"

At my blank look, Mrs. Goldwyn steps in:

"What Mr. Goldwyn means is have you made any verbal pledges?"

I don't believe so but I'm not sure, which prompts a call to Blanche.

"I have your young man here," Goldwyn tells her. "We've been talking and he seems a decent sort."

Blanche assures him we've made no commitments of any kind.

Eyeing me, he tells Blanche he hopes I'm not the sort whose main concern is getting a weekly paycheck.

"I like writers," he assures. "I like to give them time to work without schedules or deadlines."

He calls Colton to be absolutely sure the property is free and clear.

Colton voices concern that in discussing *The Last Notch* I might express ideas that Goldwyn will later claim as his own.

"Anything we talk about belongs to the boy free and clear." Goldwyn vows.

For the next half hour we discuss how the television play might be expanded to a film.

As we talk, it becomes clear he hasn't read the script.

When he makes a suggestion that negates the basic premise of my story, I turn to Mrs. Goldwyn who gives me a look conveying she knows he's wrong and will explain it to him later.

Meeting adjourned.

◆ ◆

Approaching the Juilliard to meet William Schuman, I recall the time, ten years ago, when I was seized by the lunatic desire to become a concert pianist.

"You aren't the sort of person I talk to across a desk," Schuman greets me. He escorts me to a chair by a coffee table.

He insists I call him Bill.

"We have the chance of producing an enduring work of art," he declares. Says he's been searching for a libretto a long time; he is certain my story is what he's been waiting for.

"There's a theme in it worthy of Dostoevski," he asserts.

He draws a set on a scratch pad.

Lyrics?

"Why don't you do them?" he invites.

When I tell him my main interest in music is jazz, he confides writing popular songs with Frank Loesser when he was young: "The only failures Loesser ever had."

Before he begins to write the music, which will take two years, he'll need assurance that in the movie sale, expected any day, I reserve opera rights.

I guarantee it.

In parting, I tell him it's the most inspiring conversation I've ever had.

Whistling and humming, I hail a cab — have all I can do not to introduce myself to the driver and tell him of my good fortune.

❖ ❖

David Susskind, TV producer and popular talk-show host, presents me with summaries of six Legal Aid Society cases: invites me to adapt the one I like best for his TV series, *Justice*.

While I read, he makes calls.

Of the six summaries only one appeals.

When I announce my choice, Susskind disapproves, citing the way the case ends.

I grant the ending doesn't work and tell him how I'd change it.

"I like it," he says. "Write it down."

"I'll have it on your desk tomorrow morning."

"Write it now," he says handing me a yellow pad and pointing to a chair.

While I write, he conducts business as though I'm invisible.

I make two false starts, stuff them in my pocket hoping he doesn't notice.

Fifteen minutes later I hand him what I've written.

He scans the pages — says he's sending them right over to the sponsor for approval.

"I think you'll be doing a lot of work for us," he appends.

Which doesn't erase the feeling I've somehow been demeaned.

◈ ◈

The summons to a second meeting with Sam Goldwyn surprises given how poorly the first one went.
   We talk in circles awaiting Mrs. Goldwyn's arrival.
   The more we talk the more apparent it becomes he still hasn't read the script, which was messengered to him.
   "The maid must have misplaced it," he says.
   His secretary buzzes to inform that Mrs. Goldwyn just called to say she wouldn't be here.
   We regard each other wordlessly.
   His hand moves deftly beneath his desk.
   His secretary enters to inform he's late for his next appointment.

◈ ◈

Good Friday.
The Last Notch hovers like an unresolved chord.
   Kirk Douglas' lawyer says he might be interested for five grand.
   Our lawyer sneers.
   The *Life* magazine spread is definitely off.
   A story editor at NBC, partial to my work, says her ex-husband would be interested in movie rights if "the big dogs fade from the bone."
   A belated item in Hedda Hopper's gossip column, reporting seven major studios bidding on *The Last Notch,* triggers a flurry of renewed interest that quickly subsides.
   I sense my daily calls to Blanche no longer welcome.
   Apropos Good Friday, and despite having abandoned Catholicism, I forgo my usual beef burger as a sacrificial offering.

❖ ❖

I join Blanche and Eddie Colton for lunch — our first encounter.

Elfin, imperturbable, he says, "It's a pleasure to meet the author of that famous script *The Last Notch.*"

If he feels guilty about failing to deliver the big sale he promised, it isn't apparent.

"I've sold more plays to the movies than anyone else," he notes matter-of-factly.

He names some of the playwrights he's represented (Williams, Inge, Sherwood): seems pleased to inform that when push came to shove, the studios demanding changes the writers abhorred, they all found arguments for taking the dough.

He says MCA has an actor, unnamed, for whom they want to purchase *The Last Notch,* which they will then try to sell as a package to a studio.

"They'll pay ten thousand dollars with conditions: They get all rights and you don't do the screenplay."

Repressing the urge to say "Shove it," I tell him I'll think it over.

"I have to know now," Colton states. "The actor has other deals cooking."

"Opera rights?"

He's sure they'll grant them.

"In your tax bracket you can keep most of it," Blanche chimes.

"What do you say?" Colton prods. "I have to call them."

Feeling as Williams, Inge, and Sherwood must have at similar moments, I say, "OK."

While he goes off to call, Blanche assures me I'm doing the right thing.

Colton rejoins us.

"Too late," he announces blithely. "The actor took another deal."

As the check for the meal arrives, Colton departs. Blanche hands it to me.

◆ ◆

David Susskind summons me: The Borden Milk Company, sponsors of *Justice,* object to the mother in my script being presented so unfavorably that it might incline women to abandon their product.

"The mother doesn't come across as an angel," I concede. "But I think I've given her a human dimension."

As I say this, I realize I'm much more invested in this project than I was aware.

Susskind recites the changes, which I refuse to make.

I figure that's the end but he sends me to meet the sponsor's lawyer accompanied by one of his aides.

En route to the lawyer's office the aide, learning we both went to Dartmouth, does everything but sing school songs in an effort to cajole me.

The Borden's lawyer greets us impassively. The aide, delegated to bring me around, makes a lame joke.

The lawyer enumerates the changes that must be made, noting it's his "bedrock position."

I tell him I'm incapable of "throwing a perfectly good story down the drain."

Susskind's aide says "You guys complement each other."

"Personally I like the script," the lawyer volunteers.

I reciprocate, saying several of the changes are justified.

The aide's face brightens.

The lawyer asks how I feel about the major change that would make the husband the villain.

"Why are fathers fair game and mothers sacred cows — no joke intended?" I inquire.

The aide laughs excessively. The lawyer's expression doesn't change.

I propose they take my name off the script and bring in another writer as long as I'm paid for what I've done so far.

The aide has an inspiration:

"If we take your name off and add a bonus, will you make the changes?"

Before I can say no, the lawyer steps in:

"You're wasting your time," he tells the aide. "We're dealing with a young man of integrity who will probably write about this some day."

"How about I buy all the Borden's milk that doesn't sell if you do the show the way I wrote it?" I propose.

The lawyer smiles wanly.

The aide looks suicidal.

I'm one of eight people at a meeting in New York of the Television Writers of America, a fledgling group that broke with the Author's League, which previously represented television writers.

Contract negotiations with the networks were going nicely and then a BOMBSHELL:

The executive secretary of TWA, a woman hired by the West Coast branch, is subpoenaed by the

Un-American Activities Committee of California. Asked if she *is* or ever *has been* a communist, she takes the fifth.

The East Coast board demands the woman be fired. The West Coast refuses. The woman won't quit. The eastern board resigns.

Which bring us to tonight's meeting in the ballroom of the Shelton Hotel.

Waiters from a noisy party next door barge in and out as if we're nonexistent.

The new East Coast president reports no progress with the networks since the Un-American Activities Committee reared its head; he asks for a strike vote to strengthen the negotiating committee's hand.

Someone points out we're considerably shy of a quorum. The president says ballots will be mailed to the membership.

"I would consider it a privilege to carry a picket sign," he proclaims.

An elderly woman rises:

"I don't care about any of this stuff," she asserts. "What I want to know is how do you get an agent."

All other interest in *Last Notch* flown, we sell it to the ex-husband of the woman who said to call "if the big dogs fade from the bone."

I get two thousand to write the screenplay and nine more if they decide to proceed within ninety days.

"You'll get your first movie credit" is the best face Blanche can put on it.

Colton is mum.

◆ ◆

I sell four TV scripts in a month allowing Ruth to stop working for the first time since she was sixteen.
One of the scripts sold to *Omnibus* has been turned down by seventeen shows, including *Omnibus*, two years ago.

◆ ◆

When Ruth and I wed there was a caveat: Come summer, Eddie Turro, boyhood friend, and I would take a long-planned trip (our first) to Las Vegas.
We're staying at The Last Frontier, one of four hotels that dot the Strip (the road from the airport to downtown) at widely separated intervals.
"I'd buy property here if I had any dough," I remark.
"No way," Eddie states categorically. "The bubble's about to burst."*

◆ ◆

Leg weary after a long session at craps, I take a seat at a roulette table in The Last Frontier casino.
A drowsy afternoon, the only player, I chat with the dealer, an older guy identified by his tag as "Joe Cherry."
I mention my uncle by marriage, Timmy Shea, was a prominent gambler in the twenties.
"I knew him well," Joe Cherry says. "His wife's name is Margaret."
Whereupon he pushes several stacks of chips at me as the ball comes to rest on a number I didn't play.

---

* Hard to believe he became a prominent realtor in later life.

❖ ❖

In the midst of rehearsal, the famously volcanic director throws one of his patented fits over a minor story point.

I tell him to spare me his "God damn performance."

He grabs my arm.

Fortunately, because I'm wearing a brace, having slipped a disc, someone intervenes.

Wondering if I used the brace to excuse cowardly behavior, I recount the incident to my father whose creed is, "Anyone lays a hand on you, sock 'em."

"Don't excite yourself," he says. "It isn't worth it."

The resignation in his voice confirms his steady decline since my mother's death that can no longer be ignored.

❖ ❖

William Schuman's hepatitis has kept us out of touch.

I call to tell him how much I enjoyed his opera *Casey at the Bat* on TV.

"One phrase runs in my mind endlessly."

"Which one?"

I sing it.

He says he'll be in touch as soon as his lawyer satisfies himself about some points including that if the opera is published *his* publisher will do it. As for the opera, he now sees it as a one-act instead of full length.

The bloom is definitely off the rose.

Was it my singing?

I complete the script derived from Ruth's brother asking us to play the daily double for him on our honeymoon.

The brother transformed to a wealthy uncle, it depicts Casey and Joe (Ruth and me) succumbing to the temptation of pocketing the winnings.

En route home from their honeymoon, Casey and Joe stop at the uncle's house prepared to say they never went to the track. The uncle's butler greets them with news the uncle died and left them his entire estate.

Blanche gives *Studio One* first crack and is informed "the agency boys" feel the ending is "immoral" because the young couple, by inheriting the uncle's money, are being rewarded instead of punished.

That Joe and Casey, their good opinions of themselves and each other destroyed, are left morally bankrupt, eludes the agency boys.

Blanche writes that Florence Britton and Felix Jackson (*Studio One* story editor and producer) "are very disappointed in the agency reaction."

Her note goes on: "Florence says she's a bit scared to approach you (don't tell her I repeated this!) but wanted me to ask you if you would be averse to changing the ending — not necessarily to a happy one, but at least a moral one. She realized full well that a change would greatly lessen the dramatic punch but thought your agile brain might come up with something. Would you?"

Almost a year to the day since I began to write *The Last Notch,* I'm back where I started: Ruth and I living in the Bronx with my failing father because I haven't sold anything in two months.

A call from Blanche who's been conspicuously quiet of late:

"The option on *The Last Notch* runs out tomorrow."

"Nice of you to remind me."

"*They're going ahead with it,*" she announces jubilantly. "*A check for nine thousand dollars is on the way.*"

Ruth and I sip crème de menthe frappes at the San Moritz after a celebratory meal.

Even Eddie Colton's 3.5 percent (despite he had nothing to do with the sale) can't tarnish the moment.

Kraft Theatre buys the script *Studio One* turned down because "the agency boys" found the end immoral.

Retitled *Run for the Money,* it's done exactly as I wrote it.

The public outcry I hoped for fails to occur.

1955

Greenwich Village — spring.

Our first apartment, 222 Sullivan Street (one hundred and twenty-five dollars a month) is a former church, denomination unknown, converted to a kitchen, bedroom, and living room with an alcove, once the altar, where we dine.

Eddie Condon's jazz club around the corner for nights when I can't sleep and have a drink at the bar wondering what people would think if they knew beneath surface apparel I wore pajamas.

Chess tables in Washington Square Park a block away.

Things looking up — witness a call from Al McCleery who invites me to adapt a story by the prominent novelist John Marquand, which will launch *Matinee Theatre:* live dramas five days a week on NBC at three PM.

I find the story ("Beginning Now") lifeless.

I ask McCleery why he chose it.

"I like it," he states emphatically.

Reasoning I can do it as well as anyone, I take the job.

When it becomes clear that no matter what I do the story is beyond resuscitation, I render it exactly as Marquand wrote it.

It airs to deservedly mediocre reviews.

Marquand sends me a letter I open with trepidation.

To my surprise it's a paean to my effort, with a P. S.: "I now believe there is hope for television as a cultural medium."

The Theatre Guild *(The U.S. Steel Hour)* calls. They've got a commitment from Alec Guinness if they can come up with a script tout de suite.

"Do you have anything that might be right for Guinness?" the story editor implores.

The possibility of working with an actor I revere is overwhelming.

I've got nothing remotely suitable but I say, "Yes."

"Can you come in tomorrow morning at eight-thirty?" he asks, the hour emphasizing his urgency.

I go through everything I've ever written including notebooks — nothing suitable.

I run Guinness films in my mind: *Kind Hearts and Coronets, Lavender Hill Mob, Man in the White Suit* to no avail.

Ruth will have to call in the morning and say I'm ill.

Predawn, half asleep, something occurs to me. I rouse Ruth.

She hears me out: grants it's a germ.

At breakfast, after my third expanded telling, she pronounces it a valid story in need of an ending.

En route to the meeting I come up with one.

At eight-thirty I'm ushered into a conference room where the heads of the Theatre Guild await.

Pleasantries brief. I'm on.

"Billy Cascade, Guinness, is half of a second-rate, husband-and-wife vaudeville dance team," I begin.

For fifteen minutes I spell out a comic murder with several twists and a surprise ending that evokes audible delight.

"How soon can you write it?" the story editor asks.

"When do you need it?"

"Monday morning," he replies.

"It's Friday," I note.

"Monday morning or we lose Guinness," one of the Guild heads intones.

Ruth and I work nonstop for seventy-two hours. She types what I write in longhand. While she grabs some sleep, I use the typewriter. And so on, till the final fade-out by dawn Monday morning.

At ten AM I deliver "A Likely Story."

They read it instantly. The verdict unanimous: I've pulled it off.

Hours later a call from the story editor:

"We've lost Guinness. The commitment we thought we had was a mix-up in communication."

They return the script with a check for one hundred dollars.

Oh boy do we need a union!

If he ever forgets his name, all he has to do is look at his shirt, tie, handkerchief, cuffs, and cuff links all monogrammed F. M.

He's here from Hollywood, a minor movie producer, seeking a cheapie rewrite.

He wants to hear my ideas before signing the agreement Blanche prepared.

The story takes place almost exclusively on a freighter. The first day we meet I tell him I know nothing about freighters. He doesn't either. I suggest he get us aboard one to educate ourselves.

"No sooner said than done," he declares and places several calls.

He likes my ideas but wants to hear more before finalizing the deal.

Day two:

He confesses, with embarrassment, he can't get us on a freighter.

Before I went into the army, I worked as a runner for a freight forwarder.

I call them. It's been twelve years but they

remember me. They have a freighter being loaded in Weehawken. We're to be there at ten AM the next day.

F. M. not entirely pleased: What sort of producer is it who must resort to a writer's connections?

What about the agreement?

"We'll wrap it up tomorrow," he assures.

Day three we cab to Weehawken.

To reach the ship we must traverse numerous railroad tracks. F. M. is hesitant.

I assure him there's no danger and lead the way to a freighter loading a locomotive that induces a sharp list.

As a ship's officer shows us around, I make notes.

Retracing our steps to the waiting taxi, we cross the George Washington Bridge and start down the West Side Highway where we become embedded in a traffic jam.

I ask about the contract.

F. M. says he'd like to hear a few more ideas when we meet tomorrow.

"We're not meeting tomorrow," I announce offering my hand, which he takes reflexively. "It's been a pleasure."

His expression as I exit the cab is almost worth three wasted days.

A call from Blanche awaits me at home. She says F. M. called in a frightful state.

"He's on his way to my office to sign the contract."

"Tell him the ship has sailed."

"We're running low," Ruth, keeper of the exchequer, informs.

Moments later the phone rings.

"Frank Gilroy?" an exuberant and familiar voice inquires.

"Yes."

"This is Gleason," the voice offers. "You know — the roly-poly guy."

It sounds like Jackie Gleason but Marty has fooled me before.

"Is that you Marty?"

"No pal," the voice responds. "It's really me — Gleason."

My God it *is* him.

"What can I do for you?"

He tells me he came up with a story that *Studio One* wants to do in which he would star.

"I asked them to recommend a writer. They said *you.*"

I ask what the idea is.

"It's about a guy in a large family who's low man on the totem pole," he recites. "The guy's a total loser supported by his brothers and sisters. The only thing the poor shlep knows is movies, which he's expert at. He gets on the "Sixty-Four Thousand Dollar" quiz show and wins the jackpot. When he exits the house for good, the family blasts him for being selfish. Then they find the sixty-four thousand dollar check, which he endorsed to them in exchange for his freedom."

"You've got a story," I acknowledge.

"Come to my place tomorrow morning and we'll wrap it up."

As we breakfast on the terrace of his penthouse, I run ideas by him.

He likes them.

I agree to deliver the first act in a week.

Business accomplished, he asks me how I feel about extrasensory perception.

"I'm skeptical but open-minded."

"You see that?" he asks pointing to a large TV console. "A guy was here the other night who levitated it a foot off the floor. I told him I'd give him a million dollars to do that on my show. The guy said he couldn't work that way."

A week later, Gleason not home, I hand the first act to his doorman.

Two hours later he calls.

"Great pal — keep going."

One week later I deliver the second and third acts.

No word for weeks.

A call from *Studio One* informs rehearsals are under way. I attend the last one.

All actors but Gleason present. The director doing the best he can absent Gleason who's in every scene.

Three hours late, Gleason sweeps in with his entourage. They take it from the top:

Gleason doesn't know his lines; he wings it nonstop. The other actors fighting for their lives in the absence of cues.

A script girl who tries to correct Gleason is rebuked. The director stands by helplessly.

Run-through complete, the entourage applauds. Gleason, like a matador after a brilliant performance, exits triumphantly.

The show, "Uncle Ed and Circumstance" (Gleason's title, which I couldn't talk him out of), airs to rave reviews.

Several critics say he triumphed over the material.

John Marquand invites Blanche and me to lunch.

In preparation, I read a profile of him published over three issues in *The New Yorker*.

His father having squandered his inheritance gambling, Marquand entered Harvard from a plebeian high school, which made him feel like an outsider. Not all that different from my getting into Dartmouth via the GI Bill and wondering if I belonged there.

He found a sense of community working on the *Harvard Lampoon* just as I did working on *The Dartmouth*.

Marquand saw action in World War I and was a correspondent in World War II.

We both tried our hands at advertising: He a copywriter at J. Walter Thomson, which he hated. I an even shorter servitude at Young & Rubicam.

Blanche and I arrive for lunch. Marquand and a comely woman, his agent, already seated.

First impression: handsome, courtly, kindly, patrician.

He repeats his praise of my adaptation of his story.

I tell him *The Late George Apley,* his Pulitzer Prize–winning novel rendered a time and place (Boston Brahmin — turn of the century) in a way I'll never forget.

He remains amiably distanced as we chat — inquires what I do when not writing.

I'm about to mention gambling when I recall that's how his father lost the family fortune, leaving Marquand with a loathing of the subject.

"I read, play games, listen to jazz."

"What are you reading currently?"

"Nathaniel West," I reply, citing *Miss Lonely Hearts* and *The Day of the Locust.*

"I'm terribly sorry," he apologizes. "I never heard of him."

When I register surprise, Marquand takes out a

pen and pad and asks me to repeat the author's name and titles.

His agent, seeking to bond us, mentions Marquand being a correspondent in World War II.

He asks where I served.

I tell him Europe — Patton's Third Army in the waning days of the war. I am about to ask about his service in World War I when I remember the profile saying he had an aversion to discussing his war experiences.

I like him. But when lunch ends I don't know any more about him than I did before — recalling *The New Yorker* profile in which the writer concludes Marquand is a man he "could never understand."

❖ ❖

Studio One buys the script I wrote for Alec Guinness.

The bad news: The role tailored for Guinness will be played by Eddie Bracken, a competent actor of modest range who, in appearance, manner, temperament, is as different from Guinness as I can conceive.

I'm called in to discuss minor script changes. The casting, a fait accompli — I keep my mouth shut.

As the meeting adjourns, the producer wonders where they might find the trained seal that figures prominently in the story.

I tell them Sharky, a vaudeville headliner, is currently playing the Palace.

The producer calls later to announce they've signed Sharky.

It's the first time an actor I recommended got the part.

❖ ❖

Waiting to pitch a story, I chat with another writer (Don Bevan, who does the caricatures at Sardi's) until we're summoned to our separate meetings.

Exiting we meet again.

He invites me to accompany him on a sentimental journey: The 48th Street Theatre, where *Stalag 17* (which he co-wrote) played, is being demolished and he wants to say good-bye.

As the wrecking ball exposes the stage to daylight, I have a sense of desecration.

❖ ❖

A television rewrite brings me to L.A. where H. N. Swanson, prominent literary agent, represents Blanche's clients on a split commission.

Swanson (Swannie henceforth) invites me to accompany him on his daily rounds so he can introduce me at the major film studios.

I arrive at the two-storey building bearing his name on Sunset Boulevard. The receptionist says he'll be with me shortly.

The magazines in the waiting room are ancient. I study the giant swordfish, in mid-leap, on the wall.

There's a dusty, aged feeling about the place I find appropriate for a man who represented Scott Fitzgerald, William Faulkner, John O' Hara, et al.

A tall man — sixtyish, dark suit, tie, white carnation in his buttonhole, strong features — enters the waiting room with a younger man, ever smiling, in his wake.

Barely pausing, Swannie introduces himself and his aide (Eddie Carter).

"Ready to go?" he barks.

Before I can reply he's out the door with Eddie and I racing to catch up.

Swannie directs me to the seat beside Eddie, who drives.

"We'll start at Metro," he announces.

What minimal sense of L.A. geography I have disappears in a maze of turns and freeways that bring us to the Thalberg Building at MGM.

Eddie waits in the car while Swannie and I sweep by the receptionists and guards to an office marked "Story Editor." Before anyone can announce us, Swannie ushers me in.

"You see this kid?" he says by way of introduction. "He and three other guys keep that whole television thing going in New York."

My effort to make a modest disclaimer is cut off by Swannie: "Tell him that story."

"What story?"

"The one you mentioned in the car."

I remind him it's just a notion but he insists.

The story editor listens dutifully.

On to 20th Century Fox.

Same deal: Swannie leads me to an office. Barges in. Introductions followed by, "This kid and three other guys keep that whole television thing going in New York." And then, "Tell him a story."

I start to repeat the one told at MGM.

"Not that one," Swannie says. "Tell him the one you had on television last week about the Mafia guy deported to his hometown in Italy."

I do as I'm told.

On to our next destination after a heated debate between Eddie and Swannie about the shortest way to studios in the valley, which I gather has been going on for twenty years.

We take the mountain route to Warners.

Same routine. Swannie's claim that three other guys and I keep television going in New York starting to sound reasonable. By the time we reach Universal, I can't think who the other three guys are.

On to Columbia. The story editor not in. Swannie introduces me to executives buttonholed in the corridor.

Last stop Paramount: same drill.

On our way out we stop at the men's room where a familiar figure, even with his back to us, stands at a urinal.

It's Alfred Hitchcock!

Swannie hails him familiarly. Hitchcock, zipping his fly, turns.

"Tell him that suspense story," Swannie orders, backing Hitchcock against the wall between two urinals so there's no escape.

From somewhere I dredge up an idea that might qualify as suspense.

Hitchcock, with the look of one who has fallen into the hands of madmen and decides it best to go along, listens to my pitch while dabbing his running nose with a handkerchief.

"What do you think?" Swannie demands.

Hitchcock mumbles something unintelligible and flees.

"We planted some good seeds," Swannie assures as they drop me off.

1956

A man I don't know approaches me at a cocktail party: *"Christ Gilroy don't hate me!"*

In mock defensive posture he identifies himself as David Davidson, who rewrote my first half-hour show.

I file his opening line for use should I ever meet the fellow whose television script I'm currently revising.

❖ ❖

Here's the letter I write to Rouse and Green after reading the shooting script of *The Last Notch* with their alterations:

> *I feel you've taken a story of proven merit and, in the name of expansion, so emasculated it that I refuse to take any credit for the screenplay.*

Here's the letter I send after a wiser head (Ruth's) prevails:

> *To catalog my criticisms now would be a waste of time for all of us. So let it stand.*

❖ ❖

Louis de Rochemont, producer of *The March of Time,** has an idea for a semi-documentary television series, *What Is Man?* Each segment to explore the life of a person with a singular occupation.

---

* A documentary of current events shown regularly in movie houses.

I pitch and sell a story about a jazz trumpeter torn between appearing at a benefit to pay for a jazz buddy's funeral (suggested by a recent benefit for Hot Lips Page, stellar trumpeter, at the Central Plaza) and a private party to pay his overdue rent.

He tries to do both.

First the benefit where by the time he gets on he's cutting it close.

As he plays, he gets carried away: chorus after chorus, necessitating a mad dash to make the bus taking the band to the party.

It's gone.

To insure authenticity, I hire Joe Thomas, a magnificent trumpet player ("underrated" usually attached to his name) to look over my shoulder.

Every few days Joe drops by to check what I've done.

Inevitably, when leaving for his afternoon gig at the Metropole, he says, "Have to do my quart" — as if whiskey were a doctor's prescription.

As the script proceeds it occurs to me that Joe, mid-forties, strong ebony handsome face, a sly smile that occasionally interrupts his normally stolid expression, could play the lead.

Lothar Wolff, the genial émigré overseeing the project, likes the idea.

Script approved. Preproduction plans in the works. Lothar calls: "The series is cancelled."

Joe, inured to disappointment, takes it better than I do.

I ask him why he doesn't teach trumpet to help make ends meet.

"I can't stand all those bad sounds," he says and goes off to do his quart.

◆ ◆

An urgent call from the Theatre Guild: They have Imogene Coca (TV comedienne superstar) committed to *The U.S. Steel Hour* if they can come up with a script. Do I have anything?

I allude to the Alec Guinness episode; I am assured Coca's commitment is rock solid.

I pitch an idea stemming from a freighter trip I took several years ago. The passengers a fascinating mix, including the governess of Haile Selassie's grandchildren, a macho Turkish army officer, an attractive girl sent abroad in the hope of ending a romance, an Italian sailor traveling as a passenger because of an injury, the son of the ship's captain (who takes one of his many children on each voyage), and last but not least, an extravagant histrionic woman typified by her shouting, "Farewell mere existence," as we departed New York. This lady to be played by Miss Coca.

"Any romance?" the story editor asks.

"Yes. She and a straitlaced Danish businessman, whom I neglected to mention, fall deliriously in love. The night before we land they look for the captain who they want to marry them. The captain, a wise old bird, sizes it up correctly as a shipboard romance and hides until we dock. At which point the romance evaporates."

"Sounds like a downer," one of the Theatre Guild honchos observes.

"Bittersweet," I assure and recount several incidents evoking laughter.

"We need it by Friday," the editor declares.

Ruth and I, in full-court press, complete the script on time.

They call Friday afternoon: They adore it.
They call Monday: They've lost Imogene Coca.
Compensation?
One hundred dollars and their gratitude.
SHAME ON ME!

◈ ◈

Two weeks after declaring I felt no need of offspring, Ruth learns she's pregnant.

I reverse engines and welcome the prospect.

Tony, named after my Italian grandfather, weighs in at seven pounds, eleven ounces. Could a crapshooter ask for more?

The night of his birth, I repair to Eddie Condon's to celebrate with several friends.

It's Tuesday, jam session night, when two outside musicians join the usual band. One of them is Joe Thomas — another fair augury.

◈ ◈

We have one hundred and twenty-five dollars in our bank account.

Ruth and Tony due home in three days, I'm scraping paint from the iron crib that attended Ruth's birth. The fumes give me a headache.

I go to Macy's and purchase a deluxe model for seventy-five bucks — which leaves us with fifty dollars and the rent due.

I'm mulling who to borrow from when *Playhouse Ninety* invites me to adapt John Marquand's bestselling novel, *Sincerely Willis Wayde.* I guess the lunch with Marquand went better than I thought.

◆　◆

Kraft Theatre buys the script written for Imogene Coca. The Coca role will be played by (brace yourself) Eva Gabor!

The night it airs I'm in Las Vegas en route home from L.A. I call Ruth to see how the show — which I'm about to view via kinescope — fared in New York where it was seen live earlier.

"Spare yourself and don't see it," she advises.

I turn off the TV and return to the casino.

Unanimously awful reviews testify to the wisdom of Ruth's counsel.

Not having seen the show, I'm impervious.

That I won a few quid helps.

◆　◆

The Fastest Gun Alive (né *The Last Notch*) starring Glenn Ford is a hit.

The many things that bother *me*, like the dance number inserted for no reason, go unnoticed.

Variety calls it "MGM's Sleeper of the Year."

After an extended first run, it comes to the Waverly Theatre in Greenwich Village.

En route with Jada, our dachshund, for his nightly romp in Washington Square Park, I brace myself as I near the Atomic Bowl where the local wise guys invariably hail me as "four eyes."

I'm by them without a crack when I hear one guy say, *"The Fastest Gun Alive* — some bomb huh?"

Turning instinctively, I find them all looking at me.

"You wrote it?" one guy asks.

"Yes," I reply and continue on my way.

While Jada frolics with the other dogs, I wonder how they know about my connection with the movie.

On the way back, I encounter a dozen habitués of the Atomic Bowl blocking my way.

"That was a TV show before it was a movie, right?" the guy who spoke to me earlier asks.

"Yes."

"I told you it was," he says to the others. And then to me: "Who wants to pay for something they already saw free?"

"What other stuff you write?" a second guy inquires.

I name several shows and suddenly it's a seminar: "Where you get your ideas?" "How long's it take to write a script?" et cetera. After ten minutes of Q and A, I'm wondering how to end it.

"Why don't you write about *us?*" one guy asks.

"I've got my eye on you," I reply and, seizing it as an exit line, start to leave.

"Write about *us?* one of them says. "Who'd believe it?"

❖ ❖

Sincerely Willis Wayde airs.
Reviews range from:

"*A drama of unusual substance . . . Peter Lawford gave a splendid performance . . . Sarah Churchill impressive.*"   The New York Times

To:

"*One of the worst* Playhouse 90s *of the season . . . Lawford a caricature . . . Churchill sophomoric.*"
                                                                Variety

I'm alternately praised for sticking to the novel and damned for taking liberties.

No word from Marquand.

◈ ◈

"I got another one for you pal."

It's Jackie Gleason. The first I've heard from him since the *Studio One* show aired.

"You're gonna love it," he enthuses. "Be at my office, the Park Central Hotel tomorrow three o'clock."

I arrive at the appointed hour and pass through a maze of offices before I reach Gleason's secretary who ushers me in to what she identifies as "the elephant room."

What greets me is Gleason behind his desk getting a haircut, manicure, and shine while the theme song of his TV show issues from a speaker behind him.

"Hi Frank. Be with you in a minute," he says.

A young man, introduced as Joe, enters: informs Jackie that the writers of *The Honeymooners* have come up with a script in which he plays the trumpet.

Indicating the trio grooming Gleason, Joe asks how much longer he's going to be.

"Soon as she clips my pinky off we're done," Gleason replies.

The manicurist, barber, and bootblack finish in a dead heat and depart. Bullets Durgom, Gleason's agent, enters. Joe, Bullets, and I take seats around the desk.

Bullets asks Jackie if he's come up with a title for the book being written about him by Jim Bishop, author of *The Day Lincoln Was Shot*.

"You Wait and See," Jackie responds.

Bullets says he doesn't get it.

"All the way through the book I'm saying, "You wait and see." It's a great title."

"I see what you mean," Bullets concedes.

The secretary enters seeking papers on Gleason's desk.

"I still like that Horatio Alger title I came up with," Jackie says.

"What was it again?" Joe inquires.

"The Immoral Horatio Alger," Gleason says. "Better yet how about *Horatio Alger in the Nineteenth Century?*

"You mean the twentieth century," the secretary says.

Gleason studiously ignores her.

Bullets asks Joe if he's going home to see his mother in Chicago for the holidays, Joe says yes. Jackie asks if his mother still plays the nags.

"I didn't know you knew Joe's mother," Bullets says.

"Know her?" Jackie laughs. "I used to date her."

"That wasn't my mother, that was my aunt," Joe says and recounts a riotous night in Chicago that ended with Jackie blotto in Joe's aunt's house.

Jackie dismisses the secretary and we proceed to business.

"There are these two angels," Jackie begins. "One played by me — the other by Art Carney. They have straw hats with the tops out for halos. Carney's the worried angel because the town is filled with sinners whose main sin is pride. The other saint, me, is happy-go-lucky — a troubleshooter who's come to town because of the bad situation."

"My name is 'Saint Emergency,' which is the title of the story. The worried saint takes me on a tour of the town to show me vice is rampant. Nobody can see these two saints. And they never have any direct control or influence because that would rule out freedom of choice, which goes against theology. The two saints go to the town hall and we learn it's the custom for the mayor to serve eleven months. The twelfth month he's removed from office so he can't influence the next election. At the moment our two saints arrive there's a big hassle about who the interim mayor should be. When they can't agree, they settle on the town bum to be played by James Barton. He's sworn in to gales of laughter and abolishes all fines and prisons. From now on if anyone breaks the law their noses will be painted black. Little by little you see more and more people with black noses. A negro brought in for bookmaking says, 'Go on paint my nose black. No one will notice.' So they paint his nose white. There's a move to impeach Barton. They try to enlist the priest but he sees the good Barton is doing by making everyone feel sorry for each other and realizing they're all in the same boat. The final twist is the two angels' noses are painted black. Fade-out. What do you think pal?"

Fearful that if I answer honestly they'll throw me out the window, I settle on old reliable:

"Interesting but not my cup of tea."

Whereupon Joe says Jackie left out some great things and repeats the story with embellishments.

I utter a variation of "not my cup of tea," which prompts Bullets to tell the story.

Again I demur, adding that I don't want to dampen their enthusiasm.

"Nobody can dampen Jackie's enthusiasm," Bullets proclaims.

"They told me not to make records. I made them," Jackie states. "I'm never wrong about a story. I feel sorry for you because this is going to be great."

"If you had George Bernard Shaw writing it, it might be great," I concede. "But I'm no Shaw."

"OK let's take Shaw," Gleason says. "Take that thing about Androcles and the fucking lion. The lion don't want to let the man go because he loves him so fucking much. That's all there is to it. But once Shaw starts with his dialogue and ideas you forget all about the fucking lion."

I repeat "I'm no Shaw" plus I've had bad luck working on things I'm not enthused about.

"I know how you feel," Jackie empathizes. "I can't fuck a broad unless my dick's up. But you keep objecting. I like your attitude. You get irritated — it's the way pearls get made."

Bullet jumps in:

"Instead of Barton, how about Jackie plays the bum like Reggie Van Gleason?"

Jackie shoots him a withering look: "What the fuck you trying to do, make a burlesque out of it?"

I ask for time overnight to think it over.

"I'm getting to him," Gleason chortles.

As I leave, Gleason says, "I'll wait for your answer tomorrow but I'm going to get in touch with some other writers."

His theme song accompanies me to the door.

1957

Financially we're in free fall: five-month-old baby, my father in a nursing home, more shows moving to L.A.

Ruth talks of getting a job.

I sit down to my typewriter with the single-minded intention of writing something that will sell to the movies.

As focused as I have ever been in my life, I start to type:

A big bird got cooped by accident in Tula, New Mexico. Victor Massonetti. Nickname none. At least nothing known to the public. Years ago when he was a young punk they threw "Bingo" at him ("Get Vic mad and bingo it's all over.") but it didn't stick. Now he was forty. It was Mister for the past ten years. Mister M. That was a lever to move things: "Mr. M says that big strong kid should get to sleep early tonight," and so a boxing title changed hands along with a lot of money. Other simple sentences could tie up a port, an industry. It was a simple sentence that drove Mister M to Tula, New Mexico.

For several hours, nonstop, afraid the thread will break if I take a leak, I keep typing. No idea what I'm going to say next until my fingers, invested with a life of their own, speak.
When I stop, I have ten pages (elite type) and no end of the story in sight.
I could write more but fear killing the goose.
For five days I repeat this routine.
On the fifth day I type:

He sat down at the table where Sally Blaine slept, took out a pad and pencil, started jotting down what had occurred for the benefit of whoever found them. In the middle of a sentence he fell asleep. This time it was for real.

THE END

Ruth types a clean copy: forty-four pages.

We debate titles — settle on *The Transfer* — and dispatch it to Blanche who forwards it to H. N. Swanson; and we pray.

❖ ❖

News from Swannie re *The Transfer* is discouraging. Ruth actively seeking employment.

At the eleventh hour the Governor calls: The Theatre Guild wants me to adapt a prize-winning story in *The Paris Review*.

"The Blue Serge Suit," by John Langdon, concerns a boy who must decide between attending high school graduation in his grandfather's suit, sure to invite ridicule, or not going when efforts to raise twelve dollars and eighty-three cents for a new suit fail.

Lest I be burned for the third time, I demand a signed agreement before I'll discuss my ideas.

The writing's a breeze: One of those rare adaptations where you can embellish and alter without violating the author's intent.

The money buys us two more months in New York.

After that, barring another reprieve, we'll have to join the mass migration to Los Angeles.

❖ ❖

I pick up my father at the nursing home.
Plus other infirmities, his memory's fading.
I drive him to a nearby town where *The Fastest Gun Alive* is playing.

As we enter the theater, I point to my name (*his* name except for the middle initial) on the lobby poster. If he comprehends, he doesn't show it.

Halfway through the movie he nods off. When he wakens, he's disoriented.

About to part at the home, I tell him to ask me if I'm having any luck.

"Luck," he echoes.

"Luck. Ask me if I'm having any."

A bell sounds.

"Dinner," he says and starts away.

"I'm *having* luck!" I call after him.

When Swannie, one of the wealthiest and most frugal people in Hollywood phones long distance you know it's significant.

"Ducks on the pond," he announces.

A prominent Hollywood writing team (Norman Panama and Mel Frank), who also produce and direct movies, are seriously interested in *The Transfer*.

Mel Frank is coming to New York where their musical *Li'l Abner* (they did the book) is running.

"He wants to meet you, see how many heads you have," Swannie informs.

"When?"

"Tomorrow — three PM — the president's office at Paramount."

My right cheek painfully swollen due to a stone in my saliva duct, I'm about to ask for a postponement when Swannie says, "Thirty grand."

I arrive at the Paramount building five minutes after three so as not to seem eager.

I give my name to the receptionist.

A stocky man identifies himself as Mel Frank. We chat inconsequentially waiting for the Paramount head to summon us.

Aware of my swollen cheek, I try to keep it away from Frank. As I turn, he turns, resulting in a clumsy pas de deux.

"Are you deaf in your right ear?" he asks.

"No."

"Well *I* am," he says. "I'm trying to keep my good ear so I can hear better. But you keep turning the same way."

I tell him about the stone in my saliva duct.

"You sure it's not mumps?" he says suspiciously.

"Positive."

The president summons us. A bit of banter and then to business:

Mel Frank says *if* they buy *Transfer* (emphasis his), Paramount will produce and Norman Panama will direct.

"I'm just here to find out what ideas you have because it needs a lot of work."

For fifteen minutes I present ideas that Frank shoots down like clay pigeons.

The Paramount head, a genial man nearing retirement, listens indifferently.

The secretary buzzes:

"Your next appointment's here."

I figure, "Good-bye thirty grand."

"How about we all meet for lunch tomorrow at Sardi's?" the president suggests.

I accept instantly.

Frank, with obvious reluctance, agrees. "Bring some for instances," he says churlishly in parting.

❖ ❖

    Arriving at Sardi's after a night spent devising new ideas ("for instances"), I'm directed to the second floor where the Paramount president has reserved a table.
    The first to arrive, I note a man alone at the next table. It's Bosley Crowther, the all-powerful movie critic of *The New York Times,* whom I've met at Blanche's.
    As I say hello, I'm pleased he remembers me before I can say my name.
    He asks what I'm doing here. I tell him who I'm waiting for and why.
    The maitre d' appears. There's been a change; my party awaits me downstairs. Crowther wishes me good luck.
    I join the Paramount president and Mel Frank who is swallowing varied colored capsules from a pill box.
    As we eat, I present my "for instances."
    In contrast to the previous day, Mel Frank offers no comment: lets me go on in a way that certifies I'm riding a dead horse.
    Dreading the moment when I have to tell Ruth I blew it, I follow Frank and the Paramount president to the cloakroom. As we wait for our coats, Bosley Crowther descends from upstairs.
    The Paramount head greets Crowther effusively; introduces him to Mel Frank who acts like an altar boy meeting the pope.
    "And this," the Paramount president says, pointing to me, "is . . ."
    ". . . You don't have to introduce me to Frank

Gilroy, one of the best young writers in New York," Crowther says. "How's my dear friend Blanche?"

I tell him Blanche is fine.

"Give her my warmest regards," Crowther says as he exits.

Mel Frank and the Paramount president regard me like a royal heir they'd failed to recognize.

Moments after I arrive home, Swannie calls: *The Transfer* is a done deal.

GOD BLESS BOSLEY CROWTHER!

❖ ❖

I'm en route (American Airlines — first class) to L.A. to write *The Transfer* screenplay: fifteen weeks, two grand a week guaranteed.

Ruth, Tony, and Jada — our dachshund — to follow when I'm settled.

I take a plastic container from under my seat and lift the lid to insure my turtles (two red-eared sliders and a painted turtle) don't suffocate.

The man beside me cranes his head to see.

"Turtles," I say, tilting the container.

He changes his seat.

❖ ❖

I check into the Garden of Allah.

A message from Norman Panama bids me welcome: says he'll pick me up at ten AM.

I go to the bar for a nightcap. It's deserted except for two men, a stool between them at the far end.

"Ever hear of *The Man in the Grey Flannel Suit?* one man says to the other.

"Sure."

"I'm Sloan Wilson, the author," the first man informs.

The other man, duly impressed, buys him a drink.

Whether he's Sloan Wilson or not, it's too embarrassing to witness. I go to bed.

❖ ❖

Early forties but younger looking, Norman Panama is funny, naïve, ingratiating. Swannie's description ("Mel's the muscle — Norman's the soul") seems apt.

As we drive to Paramount, Norman tells me that after years of collaborating with Mel, they, at the urging of their wives and psychiatrists are embarking on separate projects while maintaining their partnership. *The Transfer* is Norman's initial attempt to go it alone.

The guard at the Paramount entrance waves us through.

Crossing the lot we encounter Bernie Feins, introduced as the story editor, flushed with excitement:

"My car broke down at the dentist. I was in a hurry so I left it there and took a bus."

When we fail to react, Feins asks Norman if he has ever taken a bus in L.A.

"No."

"Nobody has," Feins gushes. *"I'm the first one."*

"How was it?" Norman inquires.

"Great," Feins says with an air of monumental achievement. *"But I wouldn't want to do it again."*

❖ ❖

Norman shows me to my office on the top floor of the Old Writer's Building. Then to his and Mel's office on the ground floor opening on a courtyard.

"They're building separate offices for Mel and me," Norman informs, apropos their new relationship. "Till they're ready, Mel's working at home."

He proposes a loose agenda: "We talk story for a few weeks. Then you write it."

His phone rings.

In the midst of a laugh-filled chat, he turns to me: "Do you mind if Danny Kaye joins us for lunch?"

◆ ◆

Danny Kaye and I are exchanging anecdotes about growing up in Brooklyn and the Bronx, when he turns to Norman:

"This guy's a character."

Norman asks if I've rented a car. When I say no, Kaye gives me the name of a place he leases from in downtown L.A.: "Tell them I sent you."

While Norman stays behind to talk to someone, Kaye and I exit the commissary where a chauffeured limo awaits, his wife, Sylvia, in the backseat.

"Get in. I'll give you a lift," he invites.

The Old Writer's Building close by, I decline. To his wife's obvious annoyance, he insists.

I tell him I need the exercise. He urges me into the car. Sylvia voices angry objection.

"Get in!" Danny commands.

The ride, twenty seconds tops, is interminable.

◆ ◆

I'm working my way through a "Houses for Rent" list: Jada a proven deal breaker.

I decide not to volunteer we have a dog as I dial the next number.

"Do you have a dog?" the woman asks without preamble.

"Yes," I say, about to hang up when she asks, "What kind?"

"A dachshund."

"Male or female?"

"Male."

"We have a female dachshund we're eager to breed," she enthuses.

Thirty minutes later, I arrive at an impressive four-storey home where Mrs. Herding, a robust aristocratic woman, greets me.

As she shows me about, she informs that her husband, Franz, a prominent architect who designed the house, must have access to the basement where he makes wine.

"No problem,"

"What's your dachshund's name?"

"We call him Jada, but his papers list him as Wood Row's Biela."

"Gerta has papers too."

Enter Mr. Herding, Franz, mid-seventies, amiably detached.

Mrs. Herding fills him in.

"Calls for a toast," Mr. Herding declares, opening a bottle of his Reisling that he pours generously into three large glasses.

"Has Jada been bred before?" Mrs. Herding asks.

"No."

"Neither has Gerta," she informs. "May they be blessed."

"He needs a problem," Norman says, referring to the hero of *The Transfer*.

"He's *got* a problem," I remind him. "He has to transport a big-time criminal hundreds of miles across a desert road to Albuquerque with the man's friends probably going to ambush him along the way."

"I mean a *personal* problem," Norman says.

"Such as?"

"Maybe his wife left him or he was a coward in the war or he has an illness no one knows about," Norman proposes.

We discuss potential problems until lunch.

Norman takes me to a table in the commissary where a dozen writers are playing a word game.

One of them invites me to join in.

I decline, saying I don't like playing games when I eat.

"He even looks like Ernie Lehman,"* someone remarks, evoking laughter.

Leaving the commissary, Norman and I walk to the DeMille Building where his and Mel's new offices, side-by-side, are nearing completion.

"Everything's identical," Norman notes as we regard them.

"Not quite."

"What's different?"

"I think the one on the right is a little wider," I observe.

Norman borrows a tape measure from one of the workmen, measures both offices twice.

"You're right," he says darkly. "Mel's is two inches bigger.

---

* Meeting Lehman, prominent screenwriter *(Sweet Smell of Success)* subsequently, I recount the incident. "I was never very popular," he says peevishly.

I'm in the four-floor house (two hundred and fifty dollars a month) we owe to Jada.

It's the day Ruth, Tony, Jada, and actress friend, Rose Gregorio, are due. I'm awakened at eight AM by the doorbell.

An impressive, nattily attired man apologizes elaborately for disturbing me; he identifies himself as Dudley, butler to the previous tenant, Lance Reventlow, renowned playboy son of the even more renowned heiress, Barbara Hutton.

"I've come to fetch Mr. Reventlow's polo balls," he announces.

As he collects the balls, he says, "Warn your cook there's something amiss with the left rear burner."

I assure him I will.

"How many will you have in help?" he inquires.

"Two," I reply. "My wife and a friend."

Dudley departs like one deceived.

◆ ◆

Week five of my fifteen-week guarantee. Norman and I still exploring problems that might be assigned to our hero.

We take a break to drive to a jewelry store on Rodeo Drive to buy a watch for his wife on their wedding anniversary.

The salesman greets Norman effusively and presents a tray of elegant watches.

Norman points to one with a price tag of eighteen hundred dollars:

"What's the best you can do?"

"Twelve hundred," the salesman says without hesitation.

Norman registers disappointment.

"For you, Mr. Panama, eleven hundred," the salesman purrs.

Norman frowns.

"One thousand," the salesman says with a note of finality.

Norman buys it.

As we exit, I openly marvel at what I've just witnessed.

"I still got screwed," Norman says. "Hey, how about our hero's a heroin addict?"

❖ ❖

Exiting the commissary, I collide with a young man on his way in.

He apologizes excessively and is gone before it registers: *That was Elvis Presley!*

I arrive home eager to tell Ruth about having had body contact with The King and find her crying in the living room.

"You can live out here with your left hand," she sobs.

As I console her, I add what she just said to my favorite lines about Hollywood:

"No matter how hot it gets during the day, there's nothing to do at night." Dorothy Parker.

"Los Angeles is a series of suburban approaches to a city that never materializes." Saul Bellow.

Et cetera.

❖ ❖

I have nine weeks left to write the screenplay — which I can't begin until we determine the hero's problem.

I suggest putting all the problems we can conceive in a hat.

"No matter which one we pick we tell the same story."

"Let's go with alcohol," Norman says. "The guy's a total boozer resurrected at the end."

"Alcohol it is," I second. "I'll start working on the screenplay tomorrow."

"We have to run the story by Mel first," Norman informs.

When I register misgivings, Norman assures it's a mere formality: phones Mel who insists we come to his house.

A maid ushers us to the pool where Mel is wrapping up a meeting with Rod Serling and director Ralph Nelson. Rod and I exchange greetings en passant.

"What have you got?" Mel asks Norman.

"Tell him," Norman says forwarding the question to me.

I start to recite the outline we'd devised when an upstairs window opens and a woman, identified as Mrs. Frank, asks Mel if he has the green pills.

Mel says yes, motions me to continue.

I'm barely launched when he weighs in with a question reflecting dissatisfaction. I begin to respond when he cuts me off:

"We'll discuss it later. Go on."

Mrs. Frank reappears: "Do you have the red pills?"

"Yes," Mel says.

I resume and reach the point where the hero's problem is introduced.

"Is that the best you can do — alcoholism?" Mel derides.

I look to Norman for support.

He regards me like we never met before.

Mrs. Frank chimes again: "What about the capsules?"

"I've got everything," Mel barks.

"My wife and I are going for a rectal exam," he explains.

Nonplussed, I look at him.

"Don't you have regular rectal exams?" he asks.

"No."

"You should," he cautions and invites me to accompany them.

I decline and proceed with my narration.

Mel's interjections more frequent and harsher, the air is leaden when I reach the end.

Norman mute, Mel launches into a scorched earth critique.

"In other words it's worthless," I interrupt.

"I didn't say 'worthless,'" Mel says. Turns to Norman, "Did I say 'worthless'?"

Before Norman can reply, I announce I'm returning the money paid me so far in exchange for all rights to my story; I head for the house where I tell the maid to call me a cab.

Norman pursues, trying to soften Mel's words.

"It's too late," I tell him as the cab arrives.

On the way home it hits me we've spent most of the twelve thousand received so far.

Dread about breaking the news to Ruth mushrooms as I near the house.

She greets me at the door:

"Norman's on the phone. The third time he's called in the last half hour.

He pleads with me to reconsider.

I tell him I'll write the script providing I never have to deal with Mel again. Norman vows that's the way it will be.

I accept but something tells me Mel will resurface.

A Matter of Pride, which I adapted from John Langdon's story ("The Blue Serge Suit") in *The Paris Review,* directed by Dan Petrie, airs to unanimously favorable reviews.

John Langdon contacts me.

Mid-forties, stocky, energetic, he has a weathered face and white hair that make him appear older. A victim of the Great Depression, his résumé is varied: merchant seaman, carnival barker, etc.

He's a serious writer who would love to dip into the commercial honeypot but so far no luck.

He gives me a copy of his published novel, *The SS Silver Spray,* which has a storm scene worthy of Conrad.

We invite him and his wife to dinner.

I sense their awe at our digs: hasten to tell them that when the current job ends we return to a modest abode in Greenwich Village.

The Langdons reciprocate: We drive to their mobile home in a rundown section of Compton where they live with three children.

I feel we're straining their resources — am reminded what awaits us if I fail.

◆ ◆

I'm halfway through the script and gaining momentum.

Norman calls.

"Ever go to the races?"

"Occasionally."

"Someone gave me box seats at Hollywood Park this afternoon. Want to go?"

The seats are in separate boxes on either side of an aisle. Mickey Rooney and George Raft close by.
No time for serious handicapping. I give the *Daily Racing Form* a cursory look and wager.
I win — Norman loses.
Second race: I win — Norman loses.
I hear Norman conversing with a dead ringer for the boxer, Two-Ton Tony Galento, who shares his box.
I lose the third but cash the next two. Norman loses all three.
I hear an angry outburst:
"What the fuck ya talking to me about horses when you don't know the first Goddamn thing?" Two-Ton Tony accuses Norman.
"I was just trying to learn," Norman says contritely and retreats to my side.
"All I did was ask him what a furlong was," Norman explains.
"It's an eighth of a mile," I inform.
Norman starts to bet my selections.
I stab two more winners. Norman recoups his losses and then some.
"Let's do this again tomorrow," he proposes.
I allude to the screenplay due in three weeks but am easily persuaded.
For four consecutive days Norman and I go to Hollywood Park and, via my selections, win.
Today, the fifth day, Norman who feels he's tapped into the mother lode, wants to go again.
I refuse despite a secret fear that in turning my back on a winning streak I may be alienating the gods.

❖   ❖

The waitress interrupts the word game at the writer's table to take orders.

I ask for a steak *extra* rare.

The steak I'm served is well done. I tell her to take it back.

As she starts away, she's stopped by Y. Frank Freeman, head of the studio.

"Where are you going with that?" he asks

"Taking it back," she informs jerking her thumb in my direction. "*He* says it's overcooked."

The commissary goes silent.

Every eye on Freeman as he relieves the waitress of the steak, and in a voice meant to resonate, says, "*I'll eat it.*"

Lest there be any doubt who the finicky writer is, the other writers all regard me. I've lost my appetite but there's no way of exiting without drawing attention.

The waitress returns with another steak more well done than the first; she sets it before me challengingly.

I accept it without complaint knowing on my deathbed I'll regret it.

I stroll the back lot: that magical place where a frontier street becomes New York City when you turn the corner. Which gives way to a fleet of World War II bombers succeeded by a hard scrabble New England farm. And then you're in Paris. And on and on.

I think of the guilt-ridden days spent playing hooky at the Park Plaza, the Loew's Paradise, and other movie theaters in the Bronx.

If I'd only known, I was preparing for my career.

◆ ◆

Norman and his wife, Marsha, invite Ruth and me to the screening of a yet-to-be-released film at their home. It's our introduction to what, for higher echelon movie people, is a standard perk.

Longtime friends of Norman's — established Hollywood hands and mates, all older than Ruth and I — take seats after drinks and buffet.

Fade in: black-and-white, shot on location, bare-bones budget, one recognizable actor. It has a raw, almost documentary, feel.

Ruth and I exchange approving glances.

Cries of "Amateur night" and "I want my money back," establish we're in the minority.

As the story, a caper, unfolds the largely hostile audience fastens on a clumsy device the director employs repeatedly to mark the passage of time. "Here we go again," chanted with mounting derision.

I sense the loudest hooters are threatened by something they can't define or duplicate.

I note the director's name: Stanley Kubrick.*

◆ ◆

I complete the screenplay with a week to spare.
Norman loves it.
The studio loves it.
Bernie Feins, the story editor, calls me to his

---

* The movie, *The Killing,* launched Kubrick's distinguished career. From a newspaper photo, I recognize him as a chess aficionado who frequented the tables in Washington Square Park where he played DuVal, a self-styled master, for twenty-five cents a game.

office to say how pleased everyone is; he asks if I'd be interested in working on Mel Frank's script *(The Jayhawkers),* which is in trouble.

Savoring the irony, I decline

To H. N. Swanson's to say good-bye.

"So you're leaving," he says disapprovingly.

"It's time to see if I'm a playwright."

"Why now when you're hot out here?"

"Because it's now or never."

I turn in the car. People come for the rented crib and television set. A cab collects us.

With the exception of Jada's coupling with Gerta, which came to naught, we depart with a sense of achievement.

We have enough money to last four months while I devote myself exclusively to playwriting.

I tell Blanche and Swannie not to call with offers.

I rent a room above the Circle in the Square Theatre (thirty dollars a month) where Jason Robards is giving the performance of a lifetime in *The Iceman Cometh* directed by Jose Quintero.

A bare room, paint peeling from cracked walls — I install a lamp, a chair and a card table on which I place my Royal portable.

No phone. No decorations. Nothing to distract me. I'm poised to write a play but there's a problem. I don't have an idea.

Seven days a week, morning to night, I hunt to no avail.

Days become weeks become months.

My back problem returns. I need two bourbons to make it home from the office.

Walking Jada in the park one night, I'm assailed

by the thought that the talent I exhibited at Dartmouth has been extinguished by a decade of writing for hire.

I sense I'm losing control — order my arms to hug a tree.

Money running out faster than expected, I figure six weeks before I must notify Blanche and Swannie I'm available.

Three play ideas occur to me simultaneously. Unable to choose, I work on all three: one in the morning, one midday, one at night.

I don't tell Ruth what I'm doing, but she, sensing extremis, orders me to cease writing for a week.

On the third day I get a call from a guy I was in the army with who is in town for a convention. He comes for supper.

As we eat, a thought occurs: What if he had saved my life during the war and, in the process, suffered an injury that was soon to prove fatal. Aware he was dying, he'd come to see if his sacrifice was worthwhile.

None of this has any connection to our actual relationship but I recognize it as a valid play idea.

My mind races: Suppose my life was miserable. Suppose I learned the purpose of his visit without his knowing. Suppose my wife and I, despite mutual loathing, played happy house to convince him his sacrifice was not in vain.

By dessert I have the through line and a title: *Who'll Save the Plowboy?*

I'm in the zone: adding several pages a day.

My goal is "Curtain Down — The End" by Thanksgiving.

I awaken with discomfort in my abdomen. Ruth urges me to take the day off (it's Sunday), but afraid of breaking the thread, I go to my office.

At noon, discomfort severe, I go to the emergency room at St. Vincent's. An intern pronounces it a stomach upset and prescribes a thick white liquid. I take some and go back to work.

By mid-afternoon no relief, I go home.

By night, pain increasing, I call Dr. Goldberg in the Bronx.

He tells me to get in a cab and come to his office immediately. Ruth finds someone to stay with Tony and we take off

The cab travels a dozen blocks when it hits me I can't make it to the Bronx.

"Take me to the nearest hospital!" I command.

New York Hospital. A cheerful Irish lady filling out my admissions form comes to "Religious preference."

"Religion?" she queries.

I abandoned Catholicism years ago, but my father's words ("Wait till you're down on all fours. You'll be glad to see a priest then.") have never left me.

"Religion?" the Irish lady repeats.

Doubled with pain, sensing this is it, I say, "None."

"None?" she says *"And you with a name like Gilroy?"*

"None. And I'm not in the mood for a religious debate."

Minutes later I'm on the operating table.

Before the anesthesia claims me, I glean my appendix is bursting.

Me and my machine gun.

Charlie Jones, waitress #7, and me (Austria, after the war): "We'll never be so free again."

You can tell we're homeward bound: I'm not even wearing a life jacket.

Ohrdruf-Nord, the first concentration camp overrun by U.S. Forces.
I vow to bear witness.

Directorate of America's oldest college newspaper.
(1949–1950)

Jam session: Is it my playing or my socks evoking those reactions?

Zuk's Castle Grill (1950): Rusty Jackman — trombone; me — cornet; Ham Carson — clarinet; Tommy Ruggles — drums; Bob Pilsbury — piano.

Toss-up: Which was worse, my playing or my singing?

Gilroy Was There

Every June, as the schools and colleges close, newspaper offices swarm with young men and women eager to try their hands at newspapering. One such who called at the Daily Eagle office, where he had to be told that there was small hope for a job, decided instead to join two friends who were planning to drive to Mexico. At our suggestion, he has written down some of his experiences and observations.—Editor.

Mexico City.

Dear Mr. Clark,

I met "Litri" last evening. Though the name may not seem familiar, I'm sure that many of New Hampshire's older girls swooned at the sight of him some years ago.

The catch is that when they sighed at Mr. Litri, they thought they were paying tribute to the sheik himself, Rudolph Valentino. It all came about when the picture "Blood and Sand" was filmed for the first time in the days of silent flicks.

"Blood and Sand," is the story of a magnificent matador. In the clinches between heroine and hero, Valentino played the role for all it was worth, but when the plot called for action sequences involving a live bull, Litri took over.

I learned this after the third or fourth beer when somebody mentioned that the modern version of the same story was being shown around the corner, which prompted Mr. Litri to tell of his screen activities.

* * *

Litri is 46 years old and sees at least ten more years of active duty ahead for himself.

"I feel very strong," he explained," and I love my profession."

Despite his parents' objections, he started at his craft when he was nine years old under the guidance of an uncle.

"But my wife doesn't mind," he smiled, "for she is also a bull fighter. She fights both from horse and foot." And then he added, "She naturally fights smaller bulls because she is a woman and this is a man's game."

Litri is a small man, and like other members of his profession whom we've met, he is modest, friendly, and sincere.

A Spaniard, he was fighting bulls in southern France when the Germans took over and for several years they forced him to perform at their command. Once free he came to Mexico where he has recently been stymied by some trouble between the Spanish and Mexican unions which stops him from fighting in the larger plazas.

* * *

Asked what he thought of the bull fighters currently exhibiting their wares in Mexico City, the old master shrugged his shoulders.

"They are valiant," he said. "Nobody can say that most of them aren't valiant. Some of them are artistic. But the big fault is that they do not perform with the joy with which Spanish fighters do."

He went on to explain that here the fighters always seem conscious of their perilous occupation which doesn't kindle the joyful spirit that attends a Spanish fight.

Further conversation brought out the facts that Litri had been the teacher of Sidney Franklin, the Brooklyn matador, and that during his lengthy career he'd suffered 18 separate wounds.

We asked him what the trouble was between the unions that stopped Mexicans from fighting in Spain and vice versa. For the first time his face took on some of the fire that you would expect in a man who had been presented gifts by kings and made millions of people cheer hysterically.

"It is foolish business this dispute," he said, "Bull fighting is an art, and for art their is no frontier."

Yours for more artists,
FRANK GILROY

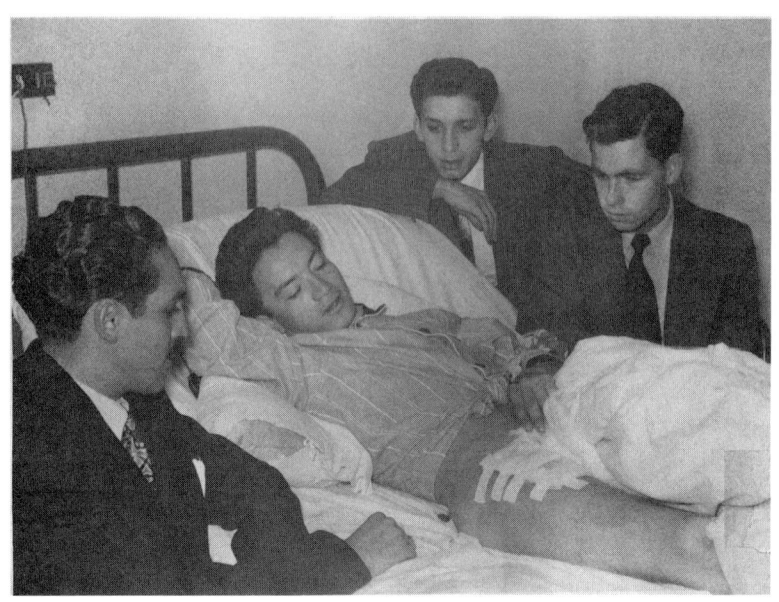

Paco Ortiz, sensation of the summer bullfighting season (1948) displaying the wound that interrupted his career to Alphonse, left, and right, the "famous American journalist."

I'm looking good until Alphonse asks them to bring out a calf for his amigo.

Blanche Gaines, my first agent, and me.
Our expressions suggest a sale.

"It's eleven-eleven. You are now man and wife."

Full-page ad in *The New York Times*. After dress rehearsal, I was glad my name was omitted.

PHOENIX THEATRE

(A Project of Theatre Incorporated) 334 EAST 74th ST. UN 1-2280

T. EDWARD HAMBLETON   NORRIS HOUGHTON

Managing Directors

presents

WHO'LL SAVE THE PLOWBOY?

A New Play by

FRANK D. GILROY

with

REBECCA DARKE   **BURTON MALLORY**   **GERALD O'LOUGHLIN**

DOROTHY PETERSON   **TOM SAWYER**   **WILLIAM SMITHERS**

Directed by DANIEL PETRIE

Costumes and Scenery by *Lighting by*
NORRIS HOUGHTON   JOHN ROBERTSON

Dan Petrie and I doing our best
to look upbeat during rehearsals.

Recovery is slow.

Too weak to go to my office, I finish *Plowboy* at home.

Initial reactions encouraging but tempered by consensus that the ending doesn't work: "barren," "bleak," "desolate" suggest the poison from my appendix leaked into my typewriter.

We're scraping bottom financially so there's no time to rewrite. I notify Blanche and Swanson I'm available.

Swannie informs that Panama and Frank have hired a new writer to work on *The Transfer*.

"So it goes in this fickle world," he observes.

He doesn't say it, but I sense I'm not the hot item I was five months ago.

Anxious days.

And then a call from Martin Manulis, producer of *Playhouse Ninety:* "Would you be interested in adapting John Marquand's novel *Point of No Return* from the play by Paul Osborn?"

I repress the urge to shout, "YOU BET YOUR ASS!"

"Your timing's impeccable," I reply. "I've just this minute completed another job."

1958

I arrive in L.A. to do rewrites on *Point of No Return*.

Checking into the Chateau Marmont I run into Dan Petrie, a director I've worked with several times and like a lot.

We bring each other up-to-date including that I've written a play.

"I'd love to read it," Dan says.

Taking a copy of *Plowboy* from my briefcase, I hand it to him.

I return from dinner after midnight — find a note in my box:

"No matter what time you come in, call me. Dan."

He greets me in pajamas.

"I love this play!" he exclaims. *"I'll give you money not to show it to anyone else!"*

I thank him from the bottom of my heart:

"I won't take money but I'll give you carte blanche to try and get it on."

Point of No Return airs.

Reviews run the gamut:

"Magnificent television."   Herald Tribune

"Thoroughly plodding."   The New York Times

Most are favorable with a few mixed:

"It might have been exciting had not the commercials broken the mood at least once every fifteen minutes."
                                                 Variety

"I had a very good time . . . But it seemed to be a different story . . . The differences almost the differences between Henry Fonda (who played the lead on Broadway) and Charlton Heston who

played it as if he were doing Moses in modern dress."   John Crosby — TV columnist

The one I like best is from an Albany paper that begins:

"John Phillips Marquand should be happy with television — and Frank D. Gilroy. Both have been good to him and his writing."

How Marquand feels I've no idea.

◆ ◆

Our fortunes again in a parlous state, I gamble (à la *Transfer*) on a story, written pell-mell, for movie sale.

Swannie reports "several nibbles — no bites." Moving to L.A. looms increasingly inevitable.

A call from David Susskind inviting me to adapt F. Scott Fitzgerald's "Last of the Belles" promises temporary relief.

I read the story several times in preparation for a meeting with the two women who run Susskind's story department. As I leave for the meeting, Ruth reminds me to be especially agreeable.

The meeting goes so well that they ask me to suggest a director. I recommend Dan Petrie.

Which makes Susskind's call that evening informing I'm fired a jolt. His editors feel we're too far apart.

Ruth in tears before I hang up.

I borrow five hundred dollars from Blanche and buy a one-way airline ticket to Los Angeles. With no idea how long it will be before I can send for them, I take leave of Ruth and Tony.

❖ ❖

Entering the Montecito Hotel, I'm greeted by a sign, "VISITORS FROM NEW YORK" listing actors, writer, directors — several of whom I know.

I've never been here before but the desk clerk greets me familiarly.

Populated by show folk of the second magnitude, rooms start at thirty-seven dollars and fifty cents a week rising to fifty dollars and more for a suite with kitchen.

Room 711 (favorable augury) is twin-bedded with bath.

I place my Royal portable on a table and position a stack of blank paper beside it. Never have I been so focused — my objective so clear: I must pass those pages through my typewriter so they emerge as gold.

Shades of Rumplestiltskin.

❖ ❖

How's our friend Mr. Kaye?" the salesman greets me.

"Danny's fine," I assure.

Thanks to Kaye, who I've had no contact with since that one meeting, I drive away in a new white Impala convertible rented at rock-bottom price.

On to 8523 Sunset Boulevard where Swannie introduces me to Jerry Perenchio, late twenties, assigned to shepherd me about till I get my bearings.

Jerry, bubbling with energy, explains the drill:

"You have an idea for a particular series, I set up a meeting with the story editor. You tell him the idea. If he likes it, you get a few hundred to write an outline.

If they like the outline, you're hired to write the script."

First stop The Zane Grey Theatre, an anthology western.

En route to the meeting, Jerry defines himself as "a flesh peddler" who's been booking bands and doesn't know beans about writing or writers. His candor and enthusiasm are appealing and infectious.

Armed with a story vastly different from their usual fare, I approach the meeting confidently.

Jerry makes the introductions and retires.

A ritual schmooze and I recite the tale of two frontiersmen, deadly enemies who meet by chance crossing the desert. Each carries a single-shot rifle. Neither wanting to shoot first and be at the mercy of the other if they miss, they squat — fifty yards apart — and converse until the sun goes down, whereupon they retreat.

I'm less than halfway when the editor's eyes glaze. "Strike one," I report to Jerry.

Driving to our next appointment I make a lightning adjustment: From several ideas I select one that's familiar with a slight twist, which qualifies it as original.

An hour later, Jerry and I are lunching (on him) in celebration of our first sale *(The Rifleman)*.

Four weeks and counting since I checked into the Montecito.

The surface of the twin bed I don't sleep in is reserved for *The Rifleman:* outline approved, script nearing completion; *Wanted Dead or Alive:* outline approved, script underway; *Have Gun Will Travel:*

outline in progress; *The Last Dance:* sold to *Studio One*, which I'm polishing.

Jerry* says, "I don't know what the hell we're doing but aren't we doing it great?"

Things couldn't be going better and then POW, right between the eyes.

I'm skimming the contract from CBS for *The Last Dance* (an original) bought by *Studio One*.

The usual legalese. I'm about to sign when I realize there's another page attached.

It's a LOYALTY OATH requiring me to swear I'm a good citizen with no allegiance to communism.

My gut tightens. I thought all that nonsense ceased when McCarthy's reign ended.

I have no connection with, or brief for, communism. So why am I so angry?

If I don't sign, it could mean the Black List and me with a wife, child, and invalid father. If I *do* sign it, I'll always regret it.

A phrase, heard years earlier, comes to mind: "Everything you do makes you more or less than you were before you did it."

My reflexive disdain for those who caved in during McCarthy's witch hunt comes back to haunt me.

I can sign without a word to anyone, but I know it will fester.

---

* He produced the first fight (Ali–Frazier) shown in movie theaters and the Billy Jean King–Bobby Riggs tennis extravaganza. Footnotes to his ultimate career as a multifaceted businessman, numbered by *Forbes* magazine among the world's prominent movers and shakers.

Informed of the situation, Swannie says, "I'll look into it."

An hour later, during which I agonize about what I'll do if push comes to shove, Swannie calls:

"It seems to be a hit-or-miss thing. Sometimes they send loyalty oaths — sometimes they don't."

His advice is to ignore it and see what happens.

I tear up the oath, send back the signed contract, and hold my breath.

◈ ◈

To hasten payment (seventeen hundred and fifty dollars), I deliver *The Rifleman* script by hand to Jules Levy, one of the producers.

Jules reads it on the spot.

"I like it," he says. "Except for three things."

He enumerates the "three things." I remind him they were *his* suggestions that I'd opposed but he insisted on.

"The next time be firmer with me," he admonishes.

◈ ◈

Having won seven hundred dollars in Vegas, I invite two couples to the West Coast debut of Mike Nichols and Elaine May at the Mocambo.

Mike, known from New York, gets me a ringside table.

Their performance, introduced by Milton Berle, is a triumph.

I pay the check.

My guests depart but I linger to congratulate Mike and Elaine as do some dozen other people (prominent Hollywood folk) who gravitate to my table where Mike and Elaine have joined me.

After several rounds of drinks, someone suggests the party continue at their home, which is unanimously approved.

Since I paid the previous check at this table, the waiter hands the new one to me. A discreet peek informs that I have just enough to cover it including a tip worthy of this august company.

The thought of divvying unthinkable, I hand the waiter the rest of my bankroll.

On to a Beverly Hills mansion for drinks, music, and scrambled eggs at dawn.

A night worth every penny.

◆ ◆

Mornings, after breakfast at Musso & Frank's, I add pages to each project in turn. Afternoons are devoted to pitching stories and house hunting. Nights I dip into the Montecito's ongoing poker game.

It's an odd sensation dealing to faces, many of them heavies you know from movies and TV (John Marley, Val Avery, et al.).

A unique feature of the Montecito is that no matter where you are, including the card game that changes venue nightly, the desk clerk always knows where to find you.

◆ ◆

I meet Charlie Schnee, a movie producer with eyes for the theater.

He likes *Plowboy* — wants to produce it. We

discuss the title role. Various names suggest themselves. But nothing grabs us.

At the Montecito pool I spot Jack Warden, superb character actor, holding forth in a group he continuously cracks up with jokes and impressions.

As he cavorts, I run *Plowboy* with him in mind.
HE'S PERFECT.
Schnee agrees.
If I approach Warden by way of his agent, it could take forever. If I contact him directly, I risk embarrassment. Biting the bullet, I pick up the phone.

> WARDEN:
> Hello.

> ME:
> Jack this is Frank Gilroy. I'm staying at the hotel. We've never met but I've written a play . . .

> WARDEN:
> . . . What room you in?

> ME:
> Seven-eleven.

> WARDEN:
> I'll be right down.

Three minutes later, he appears. A brief chat and, play in hand, he goes off.
Two hour later he calls:
"I want to do it."
Be still my heart.

❖ ❖

I find a house in the Palisades for three hundred and fifty dollars a month, first and last months prepaid.

I've earned over three grand but most of it's not due for weeks.

I ask Swannie for an advance. He writes a check with conspicuous reluctance, directs me to his bank.

The cashier regards the check, excuses himself, and consults a superior who announces he's going to call Mr. Swanson, as if that might scare me off.

My bona fides established, the cashier counts out one thousand dollars.

As he hands me the money, I ask what all the hugger-mugger was about.

Indicating "personal loan" inscribed on the check, he says, "It's the first loan Mr. Swanson's ever made."

Norman Panama is such an appealing guy that I can't help liking him despite *The Transfer*.

He sends me a copy of the shooting script — which bears no resemblance to what I wrote. Even the central plot point and title have been changed.

Lunching at Lucey's he offers me story credit, which I decline.

"Maybe someday we'll make *your* version," he says in his naïve way.

A man stops at the table.

Norman introduces me to Jess Oppenheimer, prominent TV producer, who exclaims, *"The Marquand man."*

When I register surprise, he informs that Marquand, unbeknownst to me, has decreed no work of his will be sanctioned for movies or television that doesn't include me as writer.

Immediately after lunch I call Blanche and Swannie, tell them I'll never do another Marquand adaptation.

A tombstone inscribed, "The Marquand man" haunts my sleep.

❖   ❖

Schnee says he phoned Jack Warden twice to set up a meeting and Warden didn't return his calls.

I call Warden, who says he never got a call from Schnee.

To salve Schnee's feelings, I tell Warden to call him.

I run into Warden who says he phoned Schnee twice and neither call was returned.

I call Schnee who says he never got a call from Warden.

Assuring them no disrespect was meant on either side, I prevail upon them to try once more.

Both report they called.

Both report their call wasn't returned.

The end.

❖   ❖

Six weeks from the day I left New York, Ruth, Tony, Jada, and I are reunited.

The house on Spoleto Drive, yellow stucco, ranch, is backed by a half-acre rose garden and bordered on one side by an avocado grove, a Japanese gardener included in the rent.

The wallpaper in Tony's room depicts nautical scenes around which I spin bedtime tales of Rindy-Bindy, a young boy who, by mischance, finds himself aboard a pirate ship.

The furnishings, the lanai especially, are overly colorful but cheery.

To top it off there's a serious library and a piano.

We get a second car, mandatory in L.A. Ruth goes from blonde to platinum. I've got more work than I can handle.

Dining with Rod and Carol Serling, who preceded us west, I announce that I feel like I'm on a permanent vacation.

"Wait till you're here six months," Rod forecasts. "You'll see it's just another lousy job."

◆ ◆

I can exhale.

The Last Dance goes on with nary a word from CBS about the loyalty oath.

Starring Dennis Hopper (James Dean acolyte) and Claire Griswold, a luminous newcomer, it's directed by John Frankenheimer.

The live broadcast is barely under way when a camera fails, akin to a plane losing an engine. Frankenheimer makes two cameras do the work of three so the loss isn't noticed.

Reviews unanimously favorable.

The one I like best *(Variety)* begins:

"There were strong overtones of F. Scott Fitzgerald in The Last Dance, *the poignant tale of a youth's hopeless, adolescent love for a rich girl which Frank Gilroy captured with tenderness and feeling."*

I'm tempted to send it to Susskind apropos "Last of the Belles," but once again Ruth prevails.

❖ ❖

Dan Petrie, in New York, keeps me posted on his efforts to get *Plowboy* produced.

As requested, he relates negative as well as positive reactions.

"Downhill all the way with no compensations," (Herb Brodkin — producer) registers indelibly.

❖ ❖

It's my first day working for Walt Disney.

Entering the parking lot, the guard says, "Good morning Frank." The personnel lady, never met before, says, "Follow me Frank — I'll show you your office."

David Harmon, a cheerful diminutive fellow, early forties, sporting a colorful vest, introduces himself noting that he and I are the only writers on the lot.

"Met Walt?" he asks.

"Not yet."

"When you do, don't call him Mr. Disney," he warns. "Everybody in the studio is on a strictly enforced first-name basis."

❖ ❖

I've been hired to write segments three and four of *Texas John Slaughter,* a new Disney TV series.

Writing tandem episodes — so each hour stands

alone but spliced together they make a movie — presents a unique challenge.

The pay is unprecedented: twelve thousand five hundred per segment. Blanche, who splits the commission with Swannie, is sure it's a mistake.

David Harmon takes me on a tour: points out street names — Pluto Lane, Ducky Alley, et cetera; shows me the field where animators play basketball and volley ball to relieve the strain and tedium of their work.

A basketball rolls in our direction. As I bend to pick it up, David restrains me. "You touch that ball, I call the Guild."

The commissary menu lists beer (another concession to animation?), which David says is verboten in all other studios.

Looking right and left to insure no one's listening, he whispers, "If we make good here, we can get back into show business."

◆ ◆

Segments three and four turned in, I await reaction.

A call summons me to Disney's office — our first meeting. He rises from a chair shaped like a saddle, greets me in a way both affable and distant.

Filling the wall behind him is what I take to be a map of the world until names register: Frontier Land, Fantasy Land, Tomorrow Land.

"Mister" forbidden, and incapable of saying "Walt," I don't call him anything.

He discusses the scripts I wrote in an informed way that amazes given the myriad projects he oversees.

His criticisms seem minor but he expresses them in an elliptical manner that leaves me uncertain and uneasy.

A call from Swanson relieves.

"Walt wants you to rewrite the first and second segments," he informs. "Twelve-five each. It's a gusher, me boy!"

◆ ◆

There's a full-court press to ready *Texas John Slaughter* (shows one and two) for shooting.

Sophie, a middle-aged secretary, is assigned to me. Her excellence and equanimity make her ideal for a rush job. Noting it takes two hours a day driving to and from Burbank, I ask if I can work at home. Highly irregular but given the rush nature of the job they agree.

Sophie gets mileage and overtime for driving to our house seven days a week. Most Saturdays and Sundays we quit work at noon. But I insist she bill them for eight hours lest I be thought sloughing.

We complete the job on time to everyone's satisfaction.

Sophie goes to Europe — a lifetime dream, previously unaffordable.

◆ ◆

Harry Keller (director), Jim Pratt (producer), and I agree that something Walt wants in the opening segment of *Texas John Slaughter* is wrong.

Walking down the long corridor to Walt's office for the meeting we requested, Harry notes the Oscars lining both walls:

"Kind of weakens our argument," he observes.

Walt listens impassively as we, with all due respect, tell him why we feel he's wrong.

Our recital concluded, Walt launches into a monologue about something unrelated. At the end of which we're dismissed.

Reprising the meeting, we conclude we've been overruled.

"From now on, we give him what he wants," Jim Pratt vows.

Harry and I concur — aware that divining Walt's intentions won't be easy.

The Gays, John and Bobby (initially actors — John turned writer), are going to Vegas for the weekend with Ruth and me.*

En route to the airport, where the Gays and Ruth await, I stop at 20th Century Fox (Swannie's suggestion) to tell David Brown, the story editor, why I'm not interested in adapting the novel he sent me.

A congenial meeting, Brown and I chat till I'm in danger of missing the plane. Picking up on my concern, Brown asks if he's keeping me from another appointment.

I tell him I'm bound for Vegas.

"Are you a gambler?" he inquires.

"Occasionally."

"What do you play?"

"Craps mostly"

---

* John Gay's numerous credits include *Run Silent, Run Deep*, *Separate Tables* (Academy Award nominee), and more mini-series television than any writer extant. His play, *Diversions and Delights* about Oscar Wilde, produced nationwide — including Broadway.

❖ ❖

"Dick Powell* needs a writer for a novel about crap shooting," he says handing me a small, red, hardcover book I promise to read over the weekend.

I barely make the plane where John Gay awaits — our wives having flown earlier because Ruth and I fly separately when Tony isn't with us.

Airborne, I open *No House Limit,* by Steve Fisher on an epigraph:

> *I have set my life upon a cast,*
> *And I will stand the hazard of the die.*
> Richard III

The prologue begins:

> *It started at exactly eleven minutes past three am on Sunday morning when Bello made his first appearance in the pit, picked up a pair of dice, and asked the house limit on bets be taken off.*

As we land in Vegas, I know, no matter what happens this weekend, I'm coming out ahead.

❖ ❖

Walt wants to discuss rewriting a segment previously approved.

Harry Keller unavailable, Jim Pratt and I approach Walt's office.

"Take notes," Jim orders, wary of Walt's vagaries.

Walt's criticism seems to be the absence of some overall ingredient.

---

* Movie musical singing star turned noirish private eye, producer, and director.

Pressed, ever so gently, for specifics, he speaks of an aunt's farm he used to visit as a boy. Punctuating his reminiscence are repeated references to the mouth-watering apple pies his aunt made.

Jim and I leave the meeting perplexed. My notes offer little guidance. It's possible Walt intended apple pie as metaphor but Jim's not taking any chances:

"I want apple pie up the kazoo," he commands.

On reading the rewritten script, in which the hero resorts to apple pie at crucial moments, Harry Keller assumes we've lost our minds.

❖ ❖

I've been paid in full for work to date so I assume the check for twelve thousand five hundred dollars, less commission, is a mistake.

"It's for the script Walt asked you to rewrite," Swannie explains. "He likes you laddie. And when Walt likes you, the sky's the limit. You've found a home."

I'm delighted by the money and pleased I enjoy Walt's favor. But the thought of growing old in his employ gives me shivers.

"What's with the Vegas novel?" I ask.

"Soon as Dick Powell's free, Brown is setting up a meeting," Swannie assures. "Meanwhile the salmon are running, so fish away."

❖ ❖

Waiting in Dick Powell's reception room, I remark on the exquisite orchid on his secretary's desk. She informs that she and her husband grow them.

The door to Powell's office opens and there he is:

that boyish, handsome face, reduced from thirty-foot screens to life-size. He tells his secretary to hold all but urgent calls and ushers me into a large rectangular room — his desk in a far corner.

His youthful demeanor erases the twenty-year difference in our ages.

I'm prepared to discuss *No House Limit* but he steers the conversation to gambling in general.

"I'm not a gambler," he volunteers. "But I'm told *you* are."

Whereupon he begins to quiz me: When did I start to gamble? What's the most I ever won or lost?

Like many nongamblers he's both fearful of, and fascinated by, the subject.

Beyond curiosity, I sense him checking my credentials and volunteer a summary starting with Lou and Macy Kay's poolroom in the Bronx where, at fifteen, I was betting baseball and horses via Whitey Rose, bookmaker in residence. On to the army at eighteen where I realized my impulsive nature was better suited to craps than cards.

A three-day crap game the centerpiece of *No House Limit,* Powell zeroes in:

"How did you do?"

I recount breaking the game going overseas on the SS *Marine Wolf* and winning big en route home aboard the *Rushville Victory.*

His secretary buzzes: "Your wife's on the phone."

Over the speaker comes the familiar sexy, husky voice of movie star June Allyson.

She's angry because the crew shooting a segment of one of his TV shows in their home has moved from the kitchen to the living room, which is strictly verboten.

I move away to give them privacy as the battle

escalates, am almost to the door when I hear Powell entreat, "Sweetheart, I'm just trying to make a buck."

It being common knowledge that Powell is one of the wealthier people in Hollywood, I assume he's being funny and turn with a smile.

His expression makes it clear he's serious.

June hangs up and we resume:

"I see the older guy in *No House Limit* like Nick the Greek or Arnold Rothstein," Powell advances.

When I agree, he asks what I know about Rothstein.

It's quiz time again. And this one's up my alley:

"Rothstein ran the biggest floating crap game in New York; he was involved in the Black Sox scandal and was killed by George McManus over a gambling debt, for which McManus was never tried," I rattle off — appending that my uncle by marriage, Timmy Shea, owned 2 percent of Rothstein's crap game.

We've barely touched on *No House Limit* but I know I've cinched the job before he says, "When can you start?"

Assignment completed to Walt's satisfaction, I'm invited to stay on.

I respectfully decline.

It's my last day at Disney before going to work for Powell at Fox.

David Harmon accompanies me to say good-bye to Harry Keller* who's directing the opening episode of *Texas John Slaughter*.

Somehow we miss the flashing red light that signals shooting in progress; we find ourselves on a

---

* Like David and me, Harry a charter member of the "Hi-be-lo-b'" weekly card game, which endured for thirty-five years.

frontier street among cowboys greeting the arrival of a stagecoach. David, wearing another one of his colorful vests, makes escaping notice impossible.

"CUT!" Harry roars.

All eyes focused on us, Harry bids cast and crew welcome *"The two meshuganah bushwackers."*

An hour later, having said good-bye to everyone but Walt, who I don't have the temerity to approach, I'm en route to my car when I encounter him in a shadowed corridor.

"I understand you're leaving," he says.

"Yes."

For what seems an eternity we stand like a father and son incapable of communicating when they part.

He mumbles something I don't catch and continues on.

I feel guilty until Harry informs that minutes after I departed Walt passed word that I was never to be allowed on the lot again.

❖ ❖

Plowboy update from Dan Petrie:

"Even the people who like it feel the ending is wrong."

I reread it and am forced to agree.

I admit I don't know how to fix it now but am certain once I hear it read, I'll know exactly what to do.

Accepting my assurance, Dan says he'll press on.

❖ ❖

In previous visits to Fox, I parked in the visitor area. Today, my first as an employee, I drive on the lot. The guard directs me to a row of small bungalows, bordering a lawn, where writers are housed.

As I make my way, observing the five-mile-per-hour limit, Fox — sprawling, no tall buildings — registers like a college campus.

My name on the door of Bungalow 13 (my number again) suggests a permanency that writers on a weekly salary, like me, don't enjoy.

Glancing down the row of bungalows I see names of prominent screenwriters topped by a playwright whose work I admire enormously: Clifford Odets.

Bungalow 13 consists of two writers' offices separated by an entrance room shared by their secretaries.

John Fante (established novelist/short story writer), compact, feisty, gregarious, some fifteen years older than me, greets me warmly. The secretaries equally welcoming.

My office consists of a sofa, an upholstered chair, and a desk on which a typewriter resides beside copies of *Daily Variety* and *The Reporter*.

I inquire about a large, ornate bungalow (vaguely gingerbread) across the lawn.

"That's the Shirley Temple cottage built especially for her when she worked here," my secretary informs.

"The guy has it now is a prick producer," Fante asserts. "Pardon the redundancy."

Joe Martin, owner of the Rainbow's End Casino in Las Vegas, refuses to pay protection to the Mob. The Mob hires a legendary gambler, Bello, to lay siege to the casino and break Joe in a marathon no-house-limit crap game.

That's the heart of the novel that Powell and I, in our first story session, agree is sound. Subplots and characters need drastic overhauling, which we also agree on.

Walking back to his office after lunch Powell has a violent coughing fit.

"Do you smoke?" he asks.

"No."

"You don't know how lucky you are," he gasps as he lights another cigarette.

We work productively and harmoniously until six PM. As I gather my papers he announces he's speaking at some function the following night:

"How about writing me some jokes?"

He says it offhandedly, but I sense a critical moment in our relationship.

"I don't write jokes," I inform in a voice intended to be amiable but firm.

Silence for an instant.

Then, expression noncommittal, he says, "See you in the morning."

◆ ◆

Fante, a fanatic golfer, challenges me to a putting contest on the lawn adjacent to our bungalow.

Indented sprinklers serve as cups. We play until someone wins ten holes.

A replenishing break, it becomes part of our daily routine. Spirited competition develops. Fante's secretary keeps a record of wins and losses to avoid dispute.

The commissary crowded, I ask a dour man, fifty-ish, seated alone, if I might join him.

He turns out to be Daniel Fuchs, author of the *Williamsburg Trilogy* — critically acclaimed novels published in the nineteen thirties.

Fuchs has lived in Hollywood, a screenwriter, for many years but seems newly arrived — out of place.

He sounds me out about my ambitions.

I tell him I'm an aspiring playwright hoping to make enough money to go back east and pursue my dream.

"You're fooling yourself," he declares with matter-of-fact certainty. "The only way you leave here is if they send you away."

Stung by his words, which conjure my worst nightmare, I intuit he blames Hollywood for not having written a novel or story in ages.

"What's to stop you right this minute from going back to your office and writing a short story?" I ask.

Bull's-eye — Achilles' heel.

"You don't understand!" Fuch fumes, dropping a five-dollar bill to pay for his half-eaten sandwich as he flees.

Because Powell abhors fade-outs and dissolves, we're trying to eliminate as many time jumps as possible.*

As we work, he occasionally hums a few bars from one of the numerous musicals he starred in. Inevitably followed by, "Remember that one?"

A few I get. Most I miss.

---

* Cutting from one scene to another not continuous in time was all but unheard of.

"You're not big for musicals," he guesses correctly.

To balance things, I mention his performance as a private eye when he switched from musicals to noir in *Murder My Sweet*. I recount seeing it during the war when we returned from a reconnaissance mission just as the movie was starting:

"When your name appeared on the screen, there was a groan because we figured another musical. Then this movie, like nothing we'd ever seen before, began."

"They liked it?"

"We loved it," I assure, offering a bad imitation of Mike Mazurski in his fanatic search for Velma.

Powell's secretary announces his agent is here. A distinguished, silver-haired, well-groomed man enters.

Powell introduces Ben Benjamin, "the best actor's agent in the business." Something about Benjamin, totally at ease, not a hint of hustle, supports Powell's opinion.

Benjamin apologizes for the intrusion but something came up he has to discuss with Powell.

I start to leave.

"Before you go, tell Ben about seeing *Murder My Sweet*," Powell directs. "And don't forget the part where you groaned."

❖ ❖

My secretary and Fante's secretary go to lunch.

I have a date off the lot; I am about to exit the bungalow when Fante, agitated, emerges from his office. He asks me to stay:

"There's a guy coming I don't want to see," he explains. "I don't know how he got on the lot but he's on his way over."

The way Fante says this implies the possibility of violence that the presence of a third party might prevent.

An overweight, muscular man, fiftyish with an implacable grin, opens the screen door without knocking.

Fante introduces us so hurriedly I miss the man's name. If my being there is a disappointment, he doesn't show it.

As they chat, I sit down to make it clear I'm waiting for Fante and have no intention of leaving without him.

The man reads the situation, tells Fante he'll see him another time, nods to me, and departs.

"What was that all about?" I ask.

"He's a golf hustler I owe money to."

Lunching with Mann Rubin, like me a New York TV writer trying to make his bones as a screenwriter at Fox, we discover a mutual admiration for the plays of Clifford Odets.

As we talk, it occurs to us that Odets, considered over the hill, would welcome a visit from two young writers who hold him in high regard.

After lunch we head for his bungalow and are almost there when questions surface:

Do we call him "mister"? How do we identify ourselves and state the purpose of our visit should his secretary ask? Suppose he sees our homage as patronizing? Suppose he tells people about these two jerks who came on to him like the Rover Boys?

What began as a pure, spontaneous impulse dies aborning.

◆ ◆

Doctor Milstein, the analyst I'm seeing, starts, yet again, to extol a novel he's reading.

I interrupt.

"You have an excellent grasp of the creative process," I grant. "But I wish you wouldn't tout any more books because I hate your taste in literature."

◆ ◆

Having decided to shift *No House Limit* from Vegas to Havana, Powell and I are flying to Cuba to check locations and make sure it's feasible. There's a revolution going on. But we're assured it's confined to the mountains and of no consequence.

Fidel Castro, the revolutionary leader, has lately taken to kidnapping celebrities and holding them for ransom. Juan Fangio, the racing car driver, one of the victims.

Reasoning that if Powell is kidnapped I'll be snatched as well, I tell Swannie to make a deal with Fox that if kidnapped, I remain on salary in exchange for Fox getting first refusal of anything I write about the experience.

I say this half jesting, but only half.

Two hours out of L.A. (a night flight to Miami where we are to change planes for Havana), we lose an engine. In that ultra calm voice reserved for such occasions, the captain announces we're putting down in El Paso.

We land without incident at two AM.

Never having traveled with a celebrity, I'm amazed how many people seek Powell's autograph and how unfailingly graciously he treats them.

With eight hours to kill till the next flight to Miami, Powell gets us a room at a nearby motel.

At four AM we're roused by a call from an El Paso reporter alerted to Powell's presence. Powell must be irritated, but his voice, as he answers perfunctory questions, doesn't betray it.

Ten AM we take off for Miami.

The plane all but empty, Powell and I take window seats — mine behind his. A stewardess asks him if I'm his son. Before he can answer, I tell her I *am* and, addressing Powell as "Dad," ask for my allowance.

It's night when we land in Havana.

The customs man attending our luggage says he did the same thing ten years earlier when Powell visited Cuba on his honeymoon. I wonder if that was with Joan Blondell or June Allyson but don't ask.

A Cuban man with an Anglo name (Williams), early forties, introduces himself as a lawyer, designated by the Battista government to guide us during our stay.

Voluble, ebullient, fluent English, Williams ushers us to a chauffeured limo that takes us to Cuba's oldest and most prestigious hotel, the Nacional.

Powell notes the deserted streets in sharp contrast to the vibrant nightlife remembered from his last visit.

"Is that because of the revolution?"

"It's television," Williams says airily. "Tomorrow you'll see the Havana you remember."

We're shown to a two-bedroom suite that, like everything else about the Nacional, has an air of faded elegance.

Williams leads us to the Nacional casino. I'm not in the mood to play but feel it incumbent to demonstrate I know my way around a crap table.

The layout differs slightly from Vegas. The size of the table differs greatly. Same width but so long that a string stretches midway that both dice must cross for a roll to be legal.

The dice cold, I lose two hundred in moments. Powell doesn't play but looks on avidly. I blow another hundred and call it quits.

Powell voices dissatisfaction that the casino offers none of the glitter found in Vegas.

"Tomorrow I'll take you to the new hotels built in the Vegas style," Williams promises.

En route to bed, the desk clerk hands Powell a note from George Raft, star actor turned greeter at one of the new casinos, asking Powell to call.

Powell crumples the note and throws it away.

◆ ◆

We waken refreshed to glorious weather.

Williams, bright-eyed and bushy-tailed, picks us up after breakfast. He's read the screenplay, pronounces it wonderful, and can't conceive of it being done anywhere but Cuba.

Powell notes how few people are staying at the Nacional.

"That's because they're going to the new places that we'll see later," Williams confides. But first he wants to show us an isolated seaside mansion that he thinks perfect for our filming needs.

We leave Havana in the chauffeured limo, travel some twenty miles when we encounter a roadblock manned by government soldiers.

The officer in charge converses with Williams.

My Spanish is minimal but the few words I pick up, plus Williams' expression, signals bad news before he informs us there's been a small hit-and-run raid by Castro.

"A minor thing but the road's closed for the time being," he says.

Back to Havana and lunch at an elegant deserted private beach club. Then to one of the new hotels where Williams takes us directly to the casino.

"A nice day like this everyone's at the beach," he says apropos the paucity of players.

One of the pit bosses tells Powell that George Raft is anxious to reach him, hands Powell Raft's phone number, which Powell pockets without reading.

I shoot craps — drop another few hundred.

Leaving the casino, Williams heads for the limo but Powell wants to see the hotel.

We tour the lobby, bars, restaurants, and pool area. Wherever we go the help outnumbers the guests.

On to another hotel and casino. Same story: few guests, I lose two hundred, another message from George Raft.

Williams' smile increasingly strained, he takes us back to the Nacional to rest up for a festive night that he's sure will allay any misgivings we have about the seriousness of the revolution.

A drive through streets even more deserted than the night before brings us to what Williams boasts is not just the biggest night club in Cuba but the hemisphere.

An avalanche of sound greets our entrance: big band Latin music, the place filled, riotous laughter, a mammoth stage where show girls and dancers cavort.

"Shades of Busby Berkley," Powell observes.

The master of ceremonies interrupts the show to introduce Powell. Spotlights converge on him to tumultuous applause. Powell takes a bow with genial aloofness.

"Do these people look like they're worried about a revolution?"

Williams exults.

Back to the Nacional casino where I try my hand again.

The shooter rolls three elevens in a row followed by several passes including lots of numbers. A hot hand at last but I'm betting *"Don't."*

Powell asks how much I've lost.

"Fifteen hundred give or take."

"I'll see that Fox reimburses you."

I decline noting, "If I won, I wouldn't give Fox a dime."

❖ ❖

It's our last day in Cuba.

Powell dismisses Williams summarily so we can wander on our own.

I ask what's with George Raft who tries to reach Powell again.

"He wants a part in our movie," Powell says — his tone conveying "not a chance."

Mid-afternoon we have drinks with the man who represents Fox in Cuba. American, late fifties, he has the detached air of one who's been abroad too long.

Powell asks about the revolution. The man says this and that but nothing definitive.

Late afternoon, sun leaking through bamboo blinds, it's like one of those English colonial movies: native uprising imminent — the last British representative holding the fort with a bottle of gin and a stiff upper lip.

Powell and I take a cab to Trader Vic's for dinner. That we're the only customers on a Saturday night speaks volumes.

Deciding he wants to stretch his legs, Powell and I walk back to the Nacional. As we pass through a dark narrow street I whisper, "If I was going to kidnap you, this is where I'd do it."

"Walk faster," he replies.

Predawn.

We're nearing L.A.

Powell voices hope that June will be at the airport to greet him.

"At three AM?"

"Yes," he says. "Won't *your* wife be there?"

"No way."

Powell scans the terminal anxiously; June's not here.

"She's not doing anything to me I didn't do to the others," he mutters enigmatically.

John Fante asks me to read a scene from the screenplay he's working on.

"I'd rather not."

"Three pages. Exposition. I just want to make sure it's clear," he presses.

Against my better judgment I read the pages: "Yes they're clear."

"What's clear?"

I recite the information the pages contain.

"Go on," Fante says with an edge.

Figuring I missed something, I offer to read the pages again but he snatches them away.

"I thought you might have something to say about the spelling and punctuation," he says sarcastically. "I worked a week on that scene."

"Exposition scenes can be tough."

"Is that a fact?" he derides. "Tell me about exposition scenes. I'm sure I'd find it instructive coming from a guy with a few television credits and one movie."

Moments later I hear him on the phone saying he's unhappy with his office and demanding immediate transfer elsewhere. By lunchtime he's gone.

I'm mystified and upset. Enter Herb Tobias — Fante's agent.

Unaware Fante moved out, Tobias admonishes me about the golf game on the lawn that is attracting attention.

"You're just starting out," he says. "If you want to get a bad reputation, that's your business. Fante can't afford it."

The mystery is solved: Fante picked a quarrel to justify moving rather than admit he was bowing to pressure.

The fun's gone but I feel compelled to play on my own. For the benefit of passersby, now perceived as hostile, I shout "FORE!"

◆ ◆

I wake up feeling great. Weather ideal. The scene I plan to write firmly in mind. Plus it's Wednesday, which means Ruth and I dine at the Santa Ynez Inn, after which she'll drop me at my weekly card game. A perfect day looms.

And then a trivial domestic dispute that escalates.

By the time I leave for the studio I'm boiling.

By the time I reach my office, the day which began so promisingly, is ruined.

Having played this scene before, I know how it will unfold: I won't be able to write. After a wasted day I'll arrive home angrier than when I left and the battle will resume. Forget about dinner at the Santa Ynez Inn. I'll drive myself to the card game where I'll play recklessly and lose. Another thing to blame her for.

And then *epiphany!*

Something said by Dr. Milstein, which meant nothing at the time, springs to mind:

"We are responsible for our own reactions."

Meaning Ruth is responsible for *her* behavior, *but* if I let it ruin *my* day, I've only myself to blame.

I complete the new scene by early afternoon, treat myself to an extended tour of Fox's back lot, arrive home upbeat. Ruth braced for battle, but I decline the gauntlet.

By the time we reach the Santa Ynez Inn, harmony reigns.

To top it all, I win at the game.

◆ ◆

Every Thursday Swannie goes from studio to studio harvesting the checks due his clients.

Occasionally on check day he invites me to lunch.

Upper-echelon writers (three grand a week and over) he takes to Scandia, a deluxe restaurant on Sunset Boulevard. Me in the fifteen-hundred-dollar category means the Fox commissary or Nibblers, where we sit at the counter and Swannie wipes the silverware meticulously with his napkin.

The creator of *College Humor,* a highly profitable magazine in the twenties, Swannie became a successful movie producer. Both jobs prelude to his true calling as a writers' representative.

In his singular devotion to writers I detect his failed attempt to be one.

Sensing my keen interest in his famous clients (Fitzgerald, Faulkner, O'Hara, Chandler, et al), Swannie relates anecdotes and incidents about them. Many involve outrageous behavior: à la Faulkner taking himself off salary when he felt a binge coming on — checking into a hotel where he drank for days with a nurse in attendance.

"I don't mind talented writers who carry on," Swannie asserts. "What I can't stand are those *un*talented ones who do it." Is that a warning?

I urge Swannie to write his memoirs lest all those great stories vanish with him. Appalled by the intimation he might be mortal, he changes the subject.*

❖ ❖

---

* Near the end of his long and distinguished career, Swannie published a slim memoir *(Sprinkled with Ruby Dust).* His opening words about me ("Frank D. Gilroy is a gambler at heart. He always has been.") are accurate. The rest is superficial and garbled suggesting he waited too long to tell his story.

The revolution seemingly stalled, Powell and I prepare a shooting script for Havana.

Daily story sessions are pleasureful and instructive: pleasureful because he reads aloud, playing all parts impressively; instructive because his unerring ear picks up clinkers previously unnoticed.

That *he's* politically conservative and *I'm* liberal is a running joke.

General Curtis LeMay, hawkish head of the U.S. Bomber Command calls from a plane, en route to L.A., to confirm a dinner date with Powell.

Powell introduces me over the speaker as one of those bleeding heart writers he has to put up with because I'm talented: The general signs off laughing.

We resume work till the chiropractor arrives with his folding table for the twice a week sessions that Powell believes are an antidote to smoking.*

1959

New Year's Day.

I awake with a hangover compounded by news that Battista fled Cuba and revolutionary forces hold sway.

Does Castro's "Freedom for everyone" mean gambling will continue?

Powell sees George Raft as our bellwether.

"If he leaves Cuba, the ship is sinking."

❖ ❖

---

* Powell died five years later, age fifty-nine, of lung cancer.

"We bet on the wrong side," Powell says by way of announcing the movie's shelved.

Four month's work come to naught is depressing.

"Get used to it," Swannie counsels. "Most of the money you'll make in this business will be from movies that never get made."

Apropos my rejoining the ranks of the unemployed, he calls me "Available Jones."

I've got an idea for a play that takes place in Vegas. Research required, I remember Powell speaking of a gambler he knew who'd offered his services when *No House Limit* was announced.

Powell gets me the Vegas address (no phone) of Bill Stubbs.

I check into the Desert Inn at noon.

My appointment with Stubbs not till three, I drive to one of the wedding chapels on the strip; I explain to the proprietor I'm doing research and ask if I might witness a ceremony.

"Perfect timing," he says. "Couple just about to tie the knot. If you'll be a witness, it will save them a few bucks."

I agree and am introduced to Arleta Beaver and the groom, whose name I miss. Middle-aged, married twenty-five years, they renew their vows in a different state every year.

The minister arrives.

Arleta opts for a recording of the ceremony: ten dollars for the first one — additional copies five dollars.

Organ music sounds.

Arleta — clutching an artificial bouquet, provided at no extra charge — the ceremony begins.

The minister reaches the point where anyone knowing why the marriage shouldn't proceed is encouraged to speak when the proprietor announces the recording apparatus wasn't turned on and we'll have to start over.

The cabdriver, serving as the second witness required to make it legal, registers displeasure till promised five bucks more.

When the ceremony ends, I ask the minister if I might have a word with him.

"Shoot," he obliges.

"Do you marry anyone and everyone who comes before you?"

"No," he says. "I draw the line at drunks. Of course with vodka they can fool you. Like last week: Everything going smooth till I asked the groom if he'd take this woman to be his wife and he roared, *You bet your ass!*"

"What's the strangest ceremony you performed?"

"I guess that would be the fellow who called me three times to marry him and this woman. Three times I showed up and three times the guy got cold feet and called it off. The fourth time he called, he swore he'd go through with it. And he did. I pronounced them man and wife. He kissed the bride then ran out of the chapel, took a cab to the Fremont Hotel where he changed into woman's clothes and jumped off the roof."

Bill Stubbs' address proves to be an isolated trailer at the junction of two dirt roads in the desert.

The woman who appears at the door, presumably Mrs. Stubbs, apologizes for his not being there: "Bill's working a double shift at the Silver Slipper."

At the Silver Slipper I ask for Stubbs, am directed to a blackjack table where he's dealing to two men — one old, one young — seated side by side.

Between deals I introduce myself.

He says he'll be off in thirty minutes.

The two players, apparently a team, bet in a way that's puzzling: small wagers hand after hand. And then for no apparent reason one or the other starts betting the limit.

Stubbs' shift ends. Over drinks I ask about what I just witnessed.

"The old guy, Smitty, has a new system," Stubbs explains. "Keeps track of what's dealt and when he thinks he has an edge, he or his partner sock it in."

"Why don't they *both* sock it in?"

"To throw people off."*

Stubbs, mid-forties, impresses as an intelligent man trapped in a life he loathes. He talks proudly of a son who displays an aptitude for science and happily shows no sign of following in his father's footsteps.

We segue from drinks to dinner. I ask about the everyday life of Vegas residents like himself. He's forthcoming but there's a bitter edge in almost everything he says.

"What's the best way to beat Vegas?" I ask.

"Bet everything on one roll. If you win, never come back."

After dinner he makes a half-hearted attempt to steer me to a friend's casino.

---

* This years before card counting surfaced suggests Smitty might have been an originator.

I decline.

We part.

I phone Ruth, six months pregnant, who had an appointment with her obstetrician.

"Are you sitting down?" she asks.

"Why?"

"We're going to have twins," she announces with trepidation because I'd often voiced an aversion to twins, reasoning it's hard enough to know who you are without having someone who looks just like you.

"*Well?*

To my surprise as well as hers, I say, *"Great."*

Taking twins as a favorable omen, I hasten to a crap table and bet all the hard ways.

◆ ◆

A weekend call from Swannie is unprecedented.

"Time to put your toys away and make me some money."

Robert Montgomery, prominent actor/director, is directing *The Gallant Hours,* a film about legendary Admiral Bull Halsey starring Jimmy Cagney.

"They've been shooting for two weeks and feel the script needs punching up," Swannie informs.

It means putting my new play aside, but the thought of working with Cagney is exciting.

Montgomery is a hard-nosed political conservative. But so was Dick Powell and we got on fine.

Swannie provides the clincher: "Two thousand a week (five hundred more than my last job) and Montgomery promises no work at night or on weekends.

I screen what's been shot so far.

What's wrong is immediately apparent: In his reverence for Halsey, whom he served under, Montgomery has striven for authenticity at the expense of drama.

His decision that there be no battle scenes compounds the problem. In black-and-white, it has a documentary feel I can't think how to alter.

And then a radical idea: Make it *more* documentary rather than *less*.

I show Montgomery a sample page:

GUADALCANAL — DAY

ADMIRAL HALSEY encounters a platoon of Marines. Stops his jeep to get their estimate of how the battle's going. As they talk the CAMERA focuses on a MARINE CORPORAL.

VOICE-OVER:
Thomas J. Howell. Born in Joplin, Missouri. Age nineteen. Better than average fastball. Great curve. He was 14 and 2 with the Louisville Colonels when he received "Greetings" from Uncle Sam. Three weeks from today a Japanese grenade will end his dream.

Montgomery likes the concept; he tells me to insert as many such vignettes as I can. That I make most of them up doesn't seem to bother anyone. Least of all the technical advisors (retired naval officers) who knock at my door repeatedly to offer assistance.

Working on a movie as it's being shot endows a screenwriter with unaccustomed power. Whatever I write is shot verbatim because there's no time for changes.

When pages I've just written are mistakenly delivered to the steno pool instead of the set, there's panic because they have nothing to film.

Despite all the pressure, Montgomery lives up to his word: no work at night or on weekends.

I conclude it's better to work for conservatives than liberals because the former, their fortunes usually made, tend to be relaxed while the latter drive you crazy with their striving. Just kidding.

◈ ◈

If this movie is in trouble, you'd never know it from watching Cagney.

Totally focused on camera, he fills the soundstage with merriment between setups.

His resemblance to Bull Halsey without makeup is remarkable. *With* makeup he and Halsey are identical twins.

When not regaling cast and crew with anecdotes, Cagney gives tap-dancing lessons — Dennis Weaver (Chester in *Gunsmoke*) who plays Halsey's aide, his most avid pupil.

Apropos my Bronx accent and learning I was a shabbas goy,* Cagney spouts Yiddish fluently.

Admiral Halsey tap dancing and speaking Yiddish blows my mind.

◈ ◈

---

* A Gentile who does things (like turning on gas and electricity) that Orthodox Jews are forbidden to do on holy days.

My aunt and her cousin visit from New York.

Showing them about MGM we encounter Montgomery who graciously chats with them at length.

As he walks away my aunt says, "It looks just like him."

◆ ◆

The real Admiral Halsey visits MGM. Hundreds of people fill a soundstage for a luncheon in his honor.

Cagney in uniform, Halsey in mufti, side by side; the former robust, the latter frail and failing, are a moving sight.

Montgomery and Cagney pay tribute to the man who played a major role in turning the tide in the Pacific.

It seems doubtful Halsey will respond but somehow he gets to his feet. His faltering voice barely audible, his words halting — Halsey speaks of the awesome burden it is to send young men to die.

I exit before the luncheon is over because if I don't get back to work, "Admiral Halsey" will have nothing to say when shooting resumes.

◆ ◆

The Gallant Hours wraps ahead of schedule.

Montgomery would like to work with me again. I mention *The Last Tycoon*, the Hollywood novel F. Scott Fitzgerald was working on when he died.

"There's no ending," Montgomery reminds.

I tell him I have a different take on that:

"Treat the novel as though Fitzgerald had finished it. And deal with what's there."

Montgomery calls Swannie, who represented Fitzgerald, about the rights.

Swannie contacts Fitzgerald's daughter and reports, "It's the last of the old homestead and she can't bear to part with it."

◆ ◆

Will I have dinner with Johnny Green, who composed "Body and Soul," "I Cover the Waterfront," "Out of Nowhere," and on and on?

My early, misplaced, ambition to be a songwriter, I eagerly accept.

I arrive at the Beverly Hills Hotel and am shown to "Mr. Green's table" where he awaits — trim, early fifties, conspicuously debonair.

He orders a martini. I order Jack Daniels.

I tell him of my attempts to be a songwriter and name most of his songs.

The waiter arrives with our drinks. Green regards his martini skeptically, rejects it because the olive is wrong.

I tell Green I heard that many, if not most, popular songs are written swiftly. He confirms this, citing "I Cover the Waterfront" that he and lyricist, Paul Francis Webster, wrote in the course of walking several blocks on Broadway.

The waiter reappears with the martini. Green still doesn't like the olive; he sends it back.

I ask how he got started. He cites "Coquette" as one his earliest successes.

"The credits read 'Guy Lombardo, Johnny Green, and Gus Kahn,' because if we didn't include

Lombardo he wouldn't have played it," Green informs, making it clear the wound hasn't healed.

The maitre d' delivers the third martini. Green rejects it.

"It's the brand of olive you prefer," the maitre d' assures.

Green orders a vodka and tonic.

He wants me to see a documentary about skiing and screen the movie *Raintree County* for which he wrote the score.

The reason he gives is fuzzy, but how can I refuse the man who wrote "Alabammy Bound," "Sentimental Journey," and sent an olive back three times.

I'm in the Shirley Temple cottage at Fox, currently the office of Jerry Wald, prolific producer said to be the inspiration for Bud Schulberg's novel *What Makes Sammy Run?*

I'm here because Wald is about to shoot *Beloved Infidel* starring Gregory Peck, based on Scott Fitzgerald's last days as recounted by gossip columnist Sheila Graham, the final love of his life.

Wald feels the screenplay, adapted from Graham's memoir, needs work.

Wald, late forties, overweight, known to be a killer-dealer, Swannie insists on being present.

"Don't give him anything till we get the ground rules set," Swannie instructs on the drive over.

Wald says he's heard good things about me. Unable to return the compliment, I merely thank him.

He wants to hear my ideas before he negotiates but Swannie is adamant. As they dicker, the door bursts open and a rangy, good-looking man, fiftyish, charges into the room.

"What the fuck are you trying to pull?" he shouts advancing on Wald who visibly cowers.

It's Sy Bartlett who wrote the screenplay.

From the tongue-lashing he gives Wald, I gather no one told him he was going to be rewritten.

"We're only talking," Wald offers lamely.

"Nothing's set."

"*It better not be,*" Bartlett threatens.

"I think you fellows better go," Wald says to Swannie and me.

As we exit, I marvel at Wald's instant capitulation and Bartlett's chutzpah.

"Wald had no choice," Swannie informs. "Peck and Bartlett are bosom buddies. If Sy complains — Peck walks."

Desilu wants me to adapt an unpublished story, written by comedian Red Skelton, into a television script.

They send me the story ornately bound in red leather with gold lettering. When I remark the elaborate cover, I'm told Skelton has many of his unpublished stories similarly bound in his library.

It's a shamelessly sentimental and implausible tale about a Mexican boy and his donkey.

The story editor a friend, I level about my assessment.

"I agree," she says. "But they're determined to do it and they'll pay top dollar."

Recalling Swannie's dictum, "For every script there's a writer who'll dance," I accept.

I read my new Vegas play to the Gays and Ruth.

Their response confirms what I suspect: close but no cigar.

Then to a matter Ruth and I have been mulling:

Would the Gays raise our children (Tony and the twins imminently due) if something should happen to Ruth and me?

They accept instantly, bonding us forever.

◆ ◆

MGM — the Thalberg building.

I'm here to convince Paul Gregory I'm the writer he should hire to adapt *God and My Country,* a novel by Mackinley Cantor.

I find the book saccharine but twins due any minute provide ample motivation.

Gregory, a genial voluptuary who produced *Night of the Hunter,* seems an unlikely choice for a movie about Boy Scouts.

He asks what I think of the book and then, before I can perjure myself, volunteers he has grave reservations.

Seizing on that, I offer an idea I'd discarded as too extreme.

"That'll reduce the sugar content," Gregory giggles approvingly.

◆ ◆

I share a two-office suite on the first floor of the Thalberg building with the writing team of Styler and Lewin.

Unlike most writing teams I've met, they *both* seem nice guys.

By the time I turn in my first pages to Gregory, the twins, Dan and John (fraternal), have entered the world and my father has departed after a lengthy illness.

Bills rolling in, I'm apprehensive about Gregory's reaction.

At two PM I'm summoned to Gregory's office.

Styler and Lewin wish me well.

Gregory loves the pages.

Returning to my office at three PM, I learn Styler and Lewin have been fired; their office vacated; their names removed from the door.

◈ ◈

From my office facing the MGM parking lot I glimpse various personages.

Today's highlights are Archie (the Mongoose) Moore, former light heavyweight champ, and Ray Bradbury, dean of science fiction writers, arguing with the parking-lot attendant about securing a space for his bicycle because he doesn't drive.

◈ ◈

The writers' table at MGM is close by the commissary entrance.

Six to eight writers, including me, lunch there most days. The youngest one at the table, I listen rapt while the elders reminisce about the golden years of A and B films when writers at each studio numbered in the hundreds.

Gary Cooper comes to the table and greets Randy MacDougall, one of our number, familiarly.

MacDougall calls him "Coop." Including us with a wave, he says, "You know the boys."

We chorus awed greetings that Cooper returns.

Enter Milton Beecher, MGM story editor, whose stop at our table is a daily occurrence.

His words are inconsequential but what he does while chatting is of great importance. If he stands behind you and rubs your shoulders, it signifies your work is meeting with approval.

Ah for the touch of Beecher's hands.

❖ ❖

Bill Bowers, who co-authored both story and screenplay of *The Gun Fighter,* one of my favorite westerns, regularly holds forth at the writers' table: He spouts anecdotes, observations, and ideas — many of which could be developed into plays or films.

One senses a story mind so rich he can't spend it fast enough.

That he's mired in Hollywood, unfulfilled, I take heed from.

❖ ❖

"Call me Ishmael."

Days when I despair of becoming a playwright (fearful I'm wasting my most productive years in Hollywood), I leave the studio on some pretext, cash a check for several hundred dollars, and go to Hollywood Park where I bet it all on whatever race is about to be run.

Win or lose, I'm momentarily distracted from my real concern.

1960

January 15.

I'm in the midst of scripting *God and My Country* when the Writers Guild of America strikes.

Like every other TV and screenwriter, I'm abruptly unemployed.

Our cause just (we seek health benefits, pension, royalties, and minimums), there's strong support and camaraderie as we take to the barricades.

❖ ❖

The money put aside to return east is going fast as the strike enters its second month.

No hint of movement on either side, I rent an office on Via de la Paz in the Palisades: furnish it with a card table, a chair, and a giant map of the solar system that meets my eye whenever I look up from my Royal portable.

It's put-up-or-shut-up time for all Hollywood writers, who, like me, have been postponing a novel or play till they had the time.

❖ ❖

The strike, in its third month, is taking a toll.

Light-hearted stories (like the writer who sought strike-fund money to meet a payment on his swimming pool) are heard no more.

What *is* heard are rumors of scabbing, supported by Warner Brothers scripts listing the writers as "W. Hermanos."

Hotels, restaurants, and other businesses feeling

the pinch blame the writers. Their accusations about all the people we're putting out of work trumpeted by the media.

Swannie has, unconscionably, laid off Eddie Carter, his right hand for twenty years.

Several fellows drop out of the card game.

Palmer Thompson, one of the writers in the card game, gets an office in the same building as mine. Each day, after lunch, we repair to the Mecca Poolroom on Fifth Street in Santa Monica.

Palmer, whose father owned a poolroom in Brooklyn, is too strong for me. To make it competitive, we switch to three-cushion billiards that neither of us have played before.

After our daily session it's back to the office and my relentless, but so far unavailing, quest for a play idea.

"Do you know how embarrassing it is to tell people they can reach you at the Mecca Poolroom?" Ruth observes.

◆ ◆

How long has the strike been going on?

When Palmer and I began to play three-cushion, we were lucky to make one billiard an hour. As of today, we're scoring fifteen regularly.

Rumors of scabbing have turned to outright denunciation. At last night's meeting, one writer knocked another down a flight of red carpeted stairs.

Independent companies are signing "favored-nations" deals — a good thing because it weakens the majors. Writers who work for those independents are envied by those, like me, scraping the bottom financially.

What's sustaining me (dare I say it?) is a play I've been working on for three weeks that seems like the genuine article.

❖ ❖

The strike in its fifth month.
A war of attrition.
The Guild calls a meeting seeking renewed support to fight on.
As one speaker after another sounds off, I sense we're heading for capitulation.
Leading the move to cave in are some of the most successful writers in Hollywood to whom health, pension, royalties, and minimums are meaningless because they have the clout to make deals that more than compensate.
The hour late. The vote near when a writer, late forties, overweight, nondescript, unknown to me, rises to speak.
His tone measured, he starts with a summary of events that brought us to this point, giving no indication which side he's on.
Then with swelling fervor, he says if we vote to continue the strike, the other side, closely watching what happens, will surrender.
Others have voiced similar sentiment but the way he puts it reawakens the spirit that made us strike in the first place.
It's as if his tongue was blessed for the occasion.
The vote to fight on passes.
The speaker's name: Sam Newman.

❖ ❖

Score one for the good guys!

June 15, five months to the day after it began, the strike ends.

We now have health, pension, royalties, and minimums.

I'm halfway through a new untitled play; we're broke — plans to return east postponed indefinitely.

Palmer and I bid fond adieu to the Mecca.

◆ ◆

We need money fast.

I pitch, sell and write two scripts for *The Rebel* TV series.

I'm conferring with Aaron Spelling, the producer, when Nick Adams, star of the show enters beside himself with laughter:

"My mother just came to L.A. by bus from New York passing out photos of me to everyone she met, saying "That's my son — the Rebel."

◆ ◆

The Gallant Hours opens.

Even critics with reservations remark its compelling authenticity:

> "Beirne Lay Jr. and Frank D. Gilroy have written a screenplay so fully packed with biographical and historical data on Admiral Halsey and his opposite number in the Japanese fleet — and likewise so loaded with characters whose names ring heroic bells — that anyone at all interested in the haunting record of the early days of the war in the South Pacific must see this film."
>
> Crowther — The New York Times

Feeling guilty that my contribution was largely fiction, I go to see it.

Montgomery and Cagney have invested it with a dedication, respect, and admiration that overwhelms my misgivings.

◆ ◆

Heigh-ho. Heigh-ho.

I'm back at MGM working on *God and My Country.*

I try working on my play as well but both projects suffer.

Art bowing to mammon, I relegate the play to weekends.

Ishmael days, when I used to go to the track, I now, for want of cash, drive to the Gays' home on D'Este Drive.

There I don a bathing suit left in their pool house (so I don't have to disturb them) and swim lap after lap until equilibrium is restored.

◆ ◆

It's ten-thirty AM.

I handed Gregory the completed draft of *God and My Country* yesterday afternoon — and still no word.

His car pulls into the parking lot at eleven: unusually late for him.

His expression approaching the Thalberg Building signals nothing.

I assume a relaxed pose, expecting him to enter without knocking at any moment.

I hear his steps go by.

At noon I go to the commissary; I take a seat at the writers' table so anyone entering can't avoid me.

No sign of Gregory by the time I finish eating, I'm about to leave when I hear Milton Beecher's voice and moments later feel his fingers kneading my shoulders.

Gregory's call after lunch to inform he loves the script is an anticlimax.

◆ ◆

Gregory and I are the flavor of the month at MGM.

They want *him* to produce and *me* to adapt *Thy Will Be Done,* a recently purchased book about the redemption and resurrection of an Episcopal priest.

One read confirms what the title and synopsis suggest: It's stillborn.

Gregory makes an unsuccessful effort to sell me.

Swannie repeats his cautionary note about fishing when the salmon run, to no avail.

◆ ◆

Mercury, Venus, Earth, Mars, Jupiter, Saturn, Uranus, Neptune, Pluto.

I'm back in my Palisades office working full-time on my play.

Swannie calls: Would I like to take a crack at *Forever,* a novel by Mildred Cram — one of those perennial properties that innumerable writers have tackled without success.

"What's it about?"

"Reincarnation," Swannie says quickly appending,

"One hour TV — fifteen thousand," before I can say, "no."

I like "one hour."

I like "fifteen thousand."

I like the challenge of trying to make something work that so many others have failed at.

❖ ❖

Add my name to the list of screenwriters fallen prey to Mildred Cram's treacly snare.

❖ ❖

"Your guy won the election last night," Dick Powell greets me as I enter his office the morning after the first Nixon/Kennedy debate.

He's summoned me because he hasn't given up on *No House Limits.* Am I available to change the locale from Havana to Estoril, Portugal, where gambling is legal?

Of course.

In parting, he remarks Nixon's five o'clock shadow cost him the presidency.

❖ ❖

October 13.

Bill Mazeroski (Pittsburgh Pirates) hits a homer in the bottom of the ninth beating the Yankees in the seventh game of the World Series.

The title *No House Limits* is changed to *Casino.*

It's my thirty-fifth birthday.

◆ ◆

No contact in months. No call to say he's coming. I'm astonished to open the front door on Paul Gregory.

"Sol Siegel loves this and he wants you to write it," Paul exclaims: "this" being a copy of *Thy Will Be Done,* which he waves.

"Siegel sent you?"

"Yes," Gregory affirms. "As a personal favor, he wants you to read it again and hopefully reconsider."

A producer coming to a writer's home is rare enough. That he's here at the behest of the studio head overwhelms better judgment.

◆ ◆

Gregory and I have been trying for two weeks to hammer out a story line on *Thy Will Be Done* when Sol Siegel summons us.

Amiable, avuncular, Siegel, whom I've not met before, seems out of place in what was once L. B. Mayer's lair.

Gregory introduces us — then, melting into the background, abandons the floor to me.

As I recount our efforts, I note blank looks from Siegel compelling me to explain things the book makes perfectly clear.

Siegel volunteers he hasn't read the book — only a synopsis.

"I guess you'd like me to read it," he offers.

"It would facilitate future discussions," I observe.

1961

Sol Siegel must have read the book because the plug is pulled on *Thy Will Be Done*. MGM offers a settlement of my fifteen week guarantee: Ten grand outright and I owe them ten weeks on a mutually agreeable property.

They have nothing "mutually agreeable" at the moment.

I resume work on my play.

◆ ◆

A message to call Dick Powell.

His television company is launching a one-hour anthology series: *The Dick Powell Theatre*. In addition to hosting each week, Powell will star in the premiere.

"You know the kind of thing I like to do," he says. "Got anything?"

My mind's a blank but I say "yes" automatically.

◆ ◆

Powell, flanked by several *Four Star* executives, says, "You're on."

What I'm selling essentially is an odd fact I stumbled on months ago: If someone phones you and you don't hang up, they can't use their phone.

Around this I spin a tale of murder that Amos Burke (Powell) a homicide detective unravels.

They like it.

They'll pay six grand, which is what all writers on the series will get.

Since Powell asked me to write it and it will be the premiere show, I feel entitled to more.

They won't budge.

I cave in.

To salve my ego, I demand series, book, and movie rights that they readily grant because it's a routine cop story with no apparent future value.

❖ ❖

Knowing the actor who's going to play the part gives a writer leeway:

What if Amos Burke, drawing on Powell's persona, is more than a routine flatfoot?

What if he's independently wealthy and commutes from his lavish home to police headquarters in a chauffeured Rolls Royce?

I try it out on Palmer who says, "You just made a million bucks."

❖ ❖

The owner of the house we've been renting for three years gives us six weeks to find new digs.

The real estate broker, sympathetic to our plight, learns that a man named Charles Hitch, who lives in Pacific Palisades, is about to be tapped by the incoming Kennedy administration as Assistant Secretary of Defense.

Hitch in a desperate hurry to get to Washington, we equally desperate, a rental deal is struck before he can list it.

Yet another reason to be grateful that Kennedy beat Nixon.

❖ ❖

Our next-door neighbor, separated by a wooden fence impossible to see over, is the songwriter Vernon Duke, whose hits include "I Can't Get Started," "What Is There to Say?" and "April in Paris."

One of our sons hits a ball over the fence into Duke's yard. When I try to retrieve it, his houseboy curtly informs he can't find it.

Duke and his wife avert their eyes whenever our paths cross.

My revenge is never playing his songs when I come upon them in the black market songbook that lists all standards in alphabetical order.

I like to think of him hearing me play "And The Angels Sing," "Angel Child," and skipping over "April in Paris," until Ruth points out that, given how poorly I play the piano, Duke might consider it a blessing.

❖ ❖

It's the worst of times.

It's the worst of times.

Ruth has major surgery.

What money we've accumulated since the strike is gone.

I remember a producer who wanted me to write for his TV series when I wasn't available. Swannie sets up an appointment.

I contrive a tale about Vegas. It's forced labor but I rely on my pitch.

For the first time in three years I fail.

I stop for a drink on my way home feeling as low as I ever have in my life.

◆ ◆

Time to play trump.

The show I wrote for Dick Powell has yet to air but advance word is bullish.

I call him:

"I have another idea you might like for your series."

On my way to *Four Star* I rehearse.

It's the same Vegas story that got shot down with minor alterations and a new title.

Skirting weak points and observing the rule, "If you can't be good, be brief," I sell it.

Six grand won't appease the wolf for long. But it's nice to know I haven't lost my curveball.

◆ ◆

We've been out here going on four years, the dream of returning east more remote than ever.

With an all-out assault, born of desperation, I complete my play.

No title having suggested itself, I comb the text. Midway in the second act a speech jumps out at me:

TIMMY:
The subject was roses.

◆ ◆

I'm sitting on a bench in a park, halfway between our house and my office, awaiting Ruth's arrival.

I gave her the play to read this morning.

We made a date to meet at one PM when she

would voice her opinion. It's now one-fifteen. Does that signal unfavorable reaction?

And then I spot her.

"I like it a lot," she greets me.

Not the rapturous words an author wants from his first reader. But given Ruth's abhorrence of superlatives it's music to my ears despite a hint of reservation.

"But?" I probe.

"I think you shortchanged the mother," Ruth says.

Like most authors met by anything but praise from their first and most trusted reader, I blow my top.

"You never did understand my work," et cetera.

I reduce Ruth to tears but she holds her ground.

I go back to my office where I rage until I hear Doctor Milstein say: "If you're so sure she's wrong, why are you mad?"

By the time I arrive home, I've outlined a new scene, practically a monologue by the mother.

Profuse apology.

Harmony restored.

Hanging over my head is the settlement on *Thy Will Be Done* that obligates me to work on "something mutually agreeable" for ten weeks at MGM.

So far they've offered nothing but dogs and cats.

Time running out before they must play or pay me, they submit three properties simultaneously.

Two have no appeal. The third — a play *(The Alligators)* by Molly Kazan, wife of the famed director — piques my interest.

That it's being produced by John Houseman* is added inducement.

◆ ◆

I report to work at MGM eager for my first meeting with Houseman.

An hour after the appointed time, I'm ushered into his office.

Sixtyish, overstuffed, innately haughty, Houseman barely acknowledges me.

I start to tell him my ideas about *The Alligators*.

"I don't have time," he informs

Enter Ethel Winant, his story editor, whom I've previously met and always gotten along with.

"In the future you'll deal with *her*," Houseman directs.

My guess is I've been forced down Houseman's throat. Any doubt erased when Ethel opens the door to a broom closet, faded furniture, musty odor, far from Houseman's suite.

"Your office," she says apologetically and flees.

◆ ◆

I've been sent to Coventry.

If I wasn't previously aware of it, Milton Beecher's glacial reception makes it clear.

Their objective is to treat me so ignominiously that I'll quit.

---

* Co-founder of the Mercury Theatre with Orson Welles and co-producer of Welles' infamous radio broadcast "War of the Worlds," Houseman's theater career was eclipsed in later life by his success as an actor in films and commercials.

What they don't know is how much I need the money plus it's the ideal place and time to write the new scene in *Roses*.

❖ ❖

I complete the new scene in two weeks, which Ruth, in her understated way, applauds.

The question now is how do I spend the remaining two months without going stir-crazy.

Except for Ethel Winant's "How's it going?" when our paths chance to cross, I've had zero contact with the Houseman office.

I read.

I stroll the studio.

I schmooze with other writers.

And then it hits me:

I'm going to work on The Alligators *and do it so well that Houseman keeps me on after the ten-week guarantee!*

❖ ❖

Herewith a smattering of hosannas that greet the airing of *Who Killed Julie Greer?*

> *"There's one thing that can be said for Dick Powell: He's a pro. And it showed last night in the style and polish that he brought to the whodunit that premiered his new anthology series."*
> The New York Times

> *"Slickly made, brightly written — one of the pleasantest hours in the new season."*
> Los Angeles Times

"*A glossy detective story which could easily be developed into an attractive weekly feature.*"
                              Associated Press

"*Who but the assuredly debonair Powell could have convincingly played a millionaire who's a full-time police inspector driving to his calls in a Rolls Royce . . . The words of Frank Gilroy's script crackle with meaning.*"   Variety

Swannie reports everyone at *Four Star* ecstatic about a series based on Amos Burke until they realized I own all rights.

"Apoplexy rampant," Swannie chortles. "Stay tuned."

❖ ❖

I'm in the sixth week of indentured service when there's a knock at my door. It's Ethel, doubtless sent by higher authorities, to insure I'm still there.

"When will you have something to show us?" she inquires.

I hand her fifty pages.

"This is a screenplay," she says.

"What did you expect?"

"An outline."

"No one requested an outline."

As she exits I say, "Don't be a stranger."

❖ ❖

A call from Dick Powell.

"How's your wife since her surgery?" "Did you get

the silver mugs I sent your twins?" "I'm closing in on a cast for *Casino*."

And then to business:

"Do you have any idea what Swanson is asking for the series rights to Amos Burke?"

"Yes."

"It's not going to happen," he warns. "You're killing the goose."

◈   ◈

Ethel stops by the writers' table.

"When do you think you'll finish?" she inquires ever so casually.

"A few weeks."

"Keep me posted," she invites.

Not a word about the first fifty pages but I know they've found favor when Beecher's attitude abruptly thaws.

◈   ◈

Good news, like bad, tends to come in bunches. Dan Petrie calls:

"The Phoenix Theatre has a three-week opening and wants to do *Plowboy*. Four weeks rehearsal starting in December. Opening January second. What do you say?"

◈   ◈

It's the last week I owe MGM.

I give Ethel another fifty pages, which brings the story to the verge of denouement.

Actually, I've written the entire script, but if they want to know how it ends, Houseman, who I haven't seen since the day we met, will have to show his hand, if not his face, by keeping me on.

"When do you expect to finish?" Ethel deadpans after reading the new pages.

"Two weeks."

"You sure?"

"I have to finish in two weeks. I have another commitment."

"OK."

MISSION ACCOMPLISHED!

◆ ◆

Friday morning of the twelfth week, on my way to lunch, I give Ethel the last twenty pages of *The Alligators*.

As I leave the commissary, Ethel intercepts me:

"Houseman wants to see you."

I follow her to the sanctum sanctorum where Houseman greets me as if we've never met.

No warmer than before, but I have his attention.

He finds my approach to *The Alligators* "interesting."

"I'll reread it over the weekend and we'll discuss it on Monday," he informs.

"I can't," I say. "As I told Ethel, I have another commitment."

"To do what?" he says in a way that suggests I'm fabricating.

"I'm having a play done in New York. I leave for rehearsals on Sunday."

At the word *play* his interest vaults.

"What play?" he says.

"It's called *Who'll Save the Plowboy?*"
"Where's it being done?"
"The Phoenix Theatre."
" I *know* the people at the Phoenix Theatre," he declares as if he's caught me in a lie and I'd best come clean.

"We open in January. If you're in New York, come see us," I invite.

The look on his face as I exit is beyond my wildest dreams.

❖ ❖

I'm on a plane to New York where *Plowboy* rehearsals begin in three days.

The man beside me asks me what I do.

If he hadn't asked, I would have found some way to tell him because I'm bursting to announce: "I'm a playwright."

The words no sooner said when the pilot announces New York fogged in and we're landing in Detroit.

I vow no more hubristic displays.

❖ ❖

I check into the Fifth Avenue Hotel.

Then to the Phoenix Theatre where Dan Petrie greets me with word that the actress who was to play the female lead bowed out.

"Don't despair," he says. "There's an actress I reserve for situations like this. She's terrible at interviews. She's awful at auditions. But she's a hell of an actress and she loves the play."

"What's her name?"

"Rebecca Darke," Dan says. "Like the male leads, Gerry O'Loughlin and Bill Smithers, she's a member of the Actors' Studio."

First a night in Detroit and now this.

I resist intimations of failure.

❖ ❖

T. Edward Hambleton and Norris Houghton, who run the Phoenix Theatre, are instantly appealing.

Amiable, gentlemanly, vaguely bumbling, wholly devoted to theater, they have a Dickensian air.

While Dan finalizes the cast and discusses the set with Houghton, I pore over the unsatisfactory *Plowboy* ending that I've vowed to correct once I hear it read.

The first reading tomorrow. I should be panicked but I've made the vow so often I believe it.

❖ ❖

Everyone has been introduced to everyone. De rigueur jollity has run its course.

The reading begins:

Rebecca Darke is nothing like the character I wrote. She's too thin. She's too short. She's too subdued. She has just one thing going for her: SHE'S WONDERFUL!

Qualities surface I never envisioned in the play.

Everything going great until the ending that proves even worse than expected.

All eyes on me.

"Give me five minutes," I announce.

Retreating to the balcony, I change a "no" to a "yes" and throw away the last two pages.

The second reading begets applause.

◆ ◆

Rehearsals going well, I take a day off to visit my aunt, uncle, and cousin in the Bronx.

It takes the promise of a heavy tip to find a cab that will venture there.

The placid streets I grew up in resemble a war zone.

My aunt and uncle aged beyond their years.

My cousin, three years older than me, crippled since birth, a wizened old man.

I ache at the thought of all the days he's been sitting there since I last saw him.

A gypsy cab returns me to my dream.

1962

New Year's Day.
Just back from rehearsal.
Did it go as poorly as I think or is it my hangover?

◆ ◆

A couple of visitors at today's rehearsal exert a pressure we're not ready for.

We move from rehearsal hall to theater tomorrow.

I find myself hoping for a miracle.

◈ ◈

The dress rehearsal is ragged but it works.

The invited audience ("Friends of the Phoenix") predisposed against the Actors' Studio cast is largely won over.

They linger — always a good sign.

Their suggestions, for the most part, are intended to make something they liked even better.

◈ ◈

The first paid preview reveals an unexpected problem: There are a lot more laughs than anyone anticipated; some of which detract from the play's intention.

The sound of laughter is so reassuring that Dan and I are pressured to make the play funnier.

Instead of adding laughs, we subtract them.

Gerry O'Loughlin hates to part with the pipe that fell out of his jacket pocket by accident, which the audience found hilarious.

◈ ◈

The second preview suggests Dan's and my gamble is paying off: The audience laughed less but felt more. The actors, following our lead, dig deeper.

I was needlessly short-tempered with Norrie.

Dan, privy to this, said he had avoided arguments with me for the sake of harmony and advised me to do the same.

Point made and conceded.

◆ ◆

I've settled on my viewing place: standing at the rear of the balcony.

During today's matinee (the best show so far), I observe an attractive, intelligent-looking woman, thirtyish, leaning forward, hands cupping her face so as not to miss a word.

No matter what the critics say, that's the review I'll treasure.

◆ ◆

The next-to-last preview dips but we seem to have a foundation below which we can't sink.

Bill Fitelson, prominent theatrical attorney, is lavish in praise:

"It's better than anything on Broadway, including *The Caretaker.*"

That's the fourth time someone has compared us favorably to *The Caretaker.*

I'm pleased because I admire *The Caretaker,* but I don't see the connection.

◆ ◆

Dan has a killer side I didn't suspect.

The actors haven't given the performance they're capable of and he pursues it relentlessly.

It's *their* baby now.

I stay as far removed as I can without appearing disinterested.

Strolling the Village, I pass an elementary school letting out. Recalling how lost I was at that age, I marvel at my journey to this moment.

❖ ❖

Opening day.

Awake since dawn.

Ruth checks the weather, says "Happy the bride . . . "

En route to the theater to drop off presents, I tell the driver he has "the most nervous man in New York" in his cab.

"Why's that?"

"I have a play opening tonight."

"What's it about?"

I tell him the story.

"Bull's-eye," he says. "You've got nothing to worry about."

I feel inordinately reassured.

❖ ❖

Full house.

Dan and I stand side by side in the balcony.

The first act is everything we hoped for.

Dan, back from intermission, reports a favorable buzz.

Act Two going even better than Act One.

We're in the stretch when Dan and I, simultaneously, note that the toy train, its movement vital to the end of the play, is derailed.

Dan buries his head in my shoulder.

Patrick O'Shaughnessy, playing the nine-year-old boy, about to exit, sees the train is off the track and calmly repositions it.

"You can look now," I tell Dan.

❖ ❖

"In its first production of a work by a new playwright the Phoenix Theatre has struck gold — a starkly taut clear-cut drama painful in its insights, poignant in its subtleties."
Crist — Herald Tribune

"With Who'll Save the Plowboy? *The Phoenix Theatre last night introduced a new playwright, Frank D. Gilroy, with a gift for the stage.*"
Taubman — The New York Times

"Mr. Gilroy *whose talents have hitherto been applied to television and the films, in* Who'll Save the Plowboy? *proves he has something to say and knows how to say it.*"
Cooke — The Wall Street Journal

"The Phoenix Theatre has at last brought us an absorbing drama by a new American playwright. It is not a pleasant play, but it is powerful, unrelenting in its naturalism and uncompromisingly honest."
Newsday

"We have a new playwright — and the title is bestowed with respect."
Nadel — World Telegram

"A bitterly drawn and fiercely honest social drama was produced at the Phoenix Theatre last night. We found it a work of high interest throughout."
Davis — Daily News

"A slice-of-life play, but in its spare and honest intensity it slices close to the center."   Time

"The Phoenix Theatre, risen once again from the ashes, has now found itself not merely a new playhouse but its first new American play in six or seven seasons. Congratulations are in order."
Tallmer — Village Voice

"After a couple of false starts the Phoenix has come up with a winner." Cue

"The play possesses a kind of dour trenchancy, as well as pity and anguish over the quirks of fate which may mark the debut of a valuable talent."
Howard Clurman — The Nation

"There are three virtues to Plowboy as precious as they are infrequent nowadays: A point of view, an accurate but not slavish literal rendering of human speech, and an unostentatious but unimpeachable integrity. It commands our pleasure and respect." John Simon — Theatre Arts

"Before very long it becomes clear that the pattern of the play is a ghost dance. A maneuvering of specters in almost mathematic relationships, a deliberate exercise in nightmare counterpoint . . . Three fine actors — William Smithers, Rebecca Darke, Gerald O'Loughlin, join director Daniel Petrie in placing unobtrusive accent upon the emptiness that lies just beyond the obvious."
Walter Kerr — Herald Tribune

"One hopes with fervor and sincerity that it will not be long before Mr. Gilroy writes another play.
Bolton — Daily Racing Form

Random House (Bennett Cerf) wants to publish *Plowboy* in hardcover.

Samuel French makes an offer for stock and amateur rights.

Blanche is besieged with foreign offers.

Congratulatory wires, letters, and phone calls pour in.

Several requests for interviews including one from the dean of New York columnists, Jimmy Breslin:

"How about I come by your hotel this afternoon at four?"

"Fine."

"It'll be a novelty talking to a playwright who isn't a fag."

"I don't want to be used like an axe."

Breslin never shows up — never calls.

◆ ◆

More wires and telegrams greet our return to L.A.

The Gays fete us with a surprise party.

What pleases most is Mrs. Vernon Duke knocking at our door with the ball that disappeared into their yard months ago.

◆ ◆

With the Gays to Ray and Maggie Bradbury's.

Among the guests, which include Eric Ambler and Joan Harrison, assistant to Alfred Hitchcock, is Norman Lloyd and his wife.

Lloyd who directed *The Golden Apple,* the first hit play the Phoenix Theatre ever had, says Houghton and T. Edward transferred it to Broadway so ineptly and with such disastrous result that it left everyone, including himself, embittered.

Cuidado hijo!

❖ ❖

Doctor Milstein thinks my irritability, withdrawal, and note taking are the usual symptoms I experience before a play idea is born.

I hope not, because if we're ever to leave here, I have to make some loot.

Transportation and hotel costs during *Plowboy* rehearsals and opening exceed what I've made in royalties.

Ruth says "One more hit and we're wiped out."

❖ ❖

It's one thing to "strike gold" as Judith Crist said of *Plowboy* in her review. It's another to mine it successfully.

Forced to vacate the Phoenix Theatre because of a prior commitment, T. Edward and Norrie move *Plowboy* to a theater on the Lower East Side where, in the absence of any serious effort to sustain it, and despite my offer to waive royalties, it closes after three weeks.

Unlike Normal Lloyd, I refuse to let it tarnish the experience or my feeling toward T. Edward and Norrie.

Ruth says it best: "They're a nonprofit theater accustomed to graceful failure. You confounded them with the possibility of commercial success."

❖ ❖

I'm working on *Kimberly,* a novel owned by Hecht-Hill-Lancaster, which everyone and his brother, including John Gay, tried their hand at during the years when HHL reigned as king of the independents.

The company dissolved because of poor choices, extravagance, and personal animosities. Harold Hecht, Jim Hill, and Burt Lancaster reunite to take one last crack at *Kimberly* that has so many script charges they will receive an enormous tax advantage if they can ever get it to the screen.

To qualify for this advantage, Jim Hill informs that the picture must be about a diamond robbery in South Africa and the lead role tailored for Burt.

He says Harold Hecht, quartered elsewhere in the Columbia building, is to be kept in the dark as much as possible.

Lancaster is never seen. But his presence hovers mightily.

◈ ◈

Driving on Wilshire I stop for a light. The car beside me honks.

It's Dick Powell. "We really should do something about Amos Burke," he says.

"I agree."

Did he say *I* should call him or that *he'd* call me as he pulled away?

◈ ◈

For five weeks Jim Hill and I try unsuccessfully to come up with a story.

I'm about to throw in the towel when the door bursts open and Burt Lancaster bounds into the room. His manner so aggressively friendly that his smile seems to precede him.

"How you guys doing?" he beams.

"Not well," I inform.

"What's the problem?"

"We've tried every variation on a diamond robbery. Nothing works."

"Why a diamond robbery?" he asks.

"Jim said that's what it has to be."

"No," Lancaster says. "It can be anything as long as it involves diamond mines in South Africa."

I look to Hill for rebuttal but he doesn't say a word.

"How about a comedy?" I venture.

"Anything means anything," Burt says in a voice brooking no further discussion.

◆ ◆

The song is ended but the melody lingers on: Rebecca Darke wins the coveted Clarence Derwent award for best performance by a nonfeatured actor or actress.

◆ ◆

Taking Burt at his word, I concoct a story about a mousy employee delegated by his firm to deliver a large dog to its wealthy owner in South Africa.

Turn of the century, beginning with a boat trip, it's an odyssey of comic misadventure and self-discovery in the diamond mines of Kimberly.

Jim Hill (briefly wed to Rita Hayworth) as cynical and romantic as anyone I've met in Hollywood, gives me a free hand — ready to say, "I told you so," if I fall on my ass.

With more than a little trepidation I hand him the first nineteen pages.

He reads them at once, pronounces them "great," and books a flight to Italy, where Burt is shooting *The Leopard,* to deliver them personally.

His parting words: "Don't tell Harold."

◆　◆

Two weeks and no call from Powell.

Increasingly aware that a weekly salary won't get me out of L.A., I call *him*.

"What are you looking for?"
"A lump sum buyout."
"How much?"
"Fifty thousand."
"Dream on."
"You name a figure."
"You won't like it."
"Try me."
"Twenty-five."
"I don't like it."
"Nice talking to you."
"Likewise."

◆　◆

I write twenty more pages while Jim's still in Italy.

Harold Hecht waylays me in a corridor.

He's read the first pages, which he likes, and tipped off there are more, demands to see them.

He is, nominally, one of my employers so I accede.

Arriving home from the studio, an hour after giving him the new pages, I find a telegram:

"GREAT WORK KEEP GOING — HAROLD"

◈ ◈

The Village Voice notifies me I'm getting an OBIE for "Best American Play of the Year."

I decide to attend the award ceremony in New York and tell Jim to take me off salary for a week.

"Would you like the names of a couple of great Greek lesbians?"

He means it.

"Thanks. But when it comes to Greek lesbians, I like to pick my own."

◈ ◈

I'm in a cab after *The Village Voice* award ceremony at which Gerald O'Loughlin, Norrie Houghton, and I won OBIES.

My nose starts to bleed from the sheer excitement of being in New York.

As I stanch the flow, I decide to accept Powell's offer.

◈ ◈

I'm about to sign the deal: twenty-five grand for letting them make a pilot plus minimum royalty.

"How'd you like to produce it?" Powell offers.

Another watershed moment.

Recalling the nosebleed, I decline.*

❖ ❖

Jim and Burt take my decision to go east and finish *Kimberly* there as a personal insult. I agree to a flat deal but sense whatever I write from now on will be DOA.

Hecht says, "I never liked it in the first place."

❖ ❖

I was thirty-two when I arrived in L.A. broke, with a wife, a son, a dog, and an unproduced play.

Five years later I'm going home momentarily solvent, with a wife (the same one), three sons, two dogs, one play produced, and a new one in my pocket.

We give ourselves a farewell party.

Certain that one eastern winter will bring us back to Shangri La, friends treat our departure as temporary.

We'll see.

THE END
(of the beginning)

---

* *Burke's Law,* Gene Barry in the title role, ran for several years. The lawsuit I initiated when they repeatedly violated the literary rights I'd expressly reserved went on for thirteen years resulting in victory and creation of new law favorable to writers, thanks to my friend and attorney, Robert Ehrenbard, whose legal acumen is only exceeded by his tenacity.

◆ POSTSCRIPT ◆

The Subject Was Roses ran for two years on Broadway providing the first line of my obit via a Pulitzer Prize . . . Jackie Gleason (1916–1987) wanted to buy it as a movie for himself. Stayed with the guys who brought me to the dance: Jack Albertson (1907–1981) who won an Oscar and a Tony, Martin Sheen, and Ulu Grosbard who directed both play and film . . . The vow I made to bear witness at Ohrdruf-Nord, the concentration camp, was fulfilled by *Contact with the Enemy,* nominated best play (1999–2000) by the Drama Desk . . . Dan Petrie (1920–2004) and I experienced the heights and depths in our working relationship but our friendship never wavered . . . It pains me to think of all the great jazz Rusty Jackman (1930–1999) denied the world by going into advertising . . . Doctor Alex Milstein, deceased, predicted that in emergency I would always resort to gambling. That I've written and sold seven gambling scripts to TV and movies in times of financial extemis bears him out . . . I forsook crap tables for making independent films (our home on the line more than once), which provided enough action for any punter . . . John and Bobby Gay still our best friends . . . Marty Donovan, who became a successful TV writer, and I still play the occasional pony — recently won our first superfecta . . . Ruth and I soon to be wed fifty-three years. She a sculptress yet to sound the depths of her proven talent — and so excellent an editor I fear she'll soon bypass me and deal with the muse directly . . . After suitably checkered careers, requisite for success in the movie business, Tony, Dan, John (fathers themselves) are respectively a writer/director, a writer, and a film editor. All three gainfully employed at the moment . . . As Ruth says, "No family should have four freelancers." . . . *Desperate Characters*, which I adapted and directed for the screen (from the novel by Paula Fox, starring Shirley MacLaine), won two Silver Bears at the Berlin Film Festival . . . I became president of the Dramatists Guild . . . I remain forever beholden to Dartmouth for opening the door . . . When I received an honorary degree from Dartmouth, a man high in the administration told reporters I was "the strangest case" they'd ever had, which I choose to interpret as a compliment . . . Inscribed on my workroom wall, where I write seven days a week, is the "Workers' Prayer" to which I wholly subscribe:

> LORD GRANT ME LABOR
> UNTIL MY LIFE IS ENDED
> AND LIFE UNTIL MY LABOR
> IS DONE.

BY THE SAME AUTHOR

FULL-LENGTH PLAYS

Who'll Save the Plowboy?
The Subject Was Roses
That Summer — That Fall
The Only Game in Town

Last Licks
Any Given Day
Contact with the Enemy

ONE-ACT PLAYS

Far Rockaway
So Please Be Kind
Come Next Tuesday
Dreams of Glory
Match Point
Give the Bishop My Faint Regards
Getting In
The Golf Ball

Present Tense
Twas Brillig
The Next Contestant
Real to Reel
A Way with Words
Fore
The Viewing
Inspector Ohms

SCREENPLAYS

The Fastest Gun Alive (with Russell Rouse)
The Gallant Hours (with Bierne Lay Jr.)
The Subject Was Roses
The Only Game In Town

SCREENPLAYS WRITTEN AND DIRECTED

Desperate Characters (from the novel by Paula Fox)
Gibbsville (from stories by John O'Hara)
From Noon Till Three
Nero Wolfe — The Doorbell Rang (from the novel by Rex Stout)
Once in Paris
The Gig
The Luckiest Man in the World
Money Plays

TELEVISION — LIVE (ANTHOLOGY)

Omnibus
The U.S. Steel Hour
Studio One
Four Star Theatre
Danger
The Lux Video Theatre
Armstrong Circle Theatre

Playhouse Ninety
Kraft Television Theatre
The Kate Smith Hour
Matinee Theatre
Revlon Summer Theatre
Gulf TV Theatre

TELEVISION — FILM (SERIES)

The Rifleman
Wanted Dead Or Alive
Texas John Slaughter
Have Gun Will Travel
The Rebel
The Dick Powell Theatre (anthology) including premier show that spawned the series *Burke's Law*.

NOVELS

Private
From Noon Till Three

CHILDREN'S BOOK

Little Ego (with Ruth Gaydos)

NONFICTION

I Wake Up Screening — Everything you need to know about making independent films including a thousand reasons not to.